Medicolegal Issues in Clinical Practice

A Primer for the Legally Challenged

Deborah J. Wear-Finkle, M.D., M.P.A.
Diplomate, American Board of Psychiatry & Neurology

Adult and Forensic Psychiatry

Rapid Psychler Press

Suite 374
3560 Pine Grove Ave.
Port Huron, Michigan
USA 48060

Suite 203
1673 Richmond St.
London, Ontario
Canada N6G 2N3

Toll Free Phone   888-PSY-CHLE (888-779-2453)
Toll Free Fax   888-PSY-CHLR (888-779-2457)
Outside the U.S. & Canada — *Phone* 519-433-7642
                                                    Fax   519-433-9130
website   www.psychler.com
email   rapid@psychler.com

ISBN 1-894328-08-6
Printed in the United States of America
Text ©2000, Deborah J. Wear-Finkle
Illustrations ©2000 Rapid Psychler Press
First Edition, First Printing

All caricatures are purely fictitious. Any resemblance to real people, either living or deceased, is entirely coincidental (and unfortunate). The author assumes no responsibility for any medical, legal, or ethical decisions made on the basis of the contents of this book. Such determinations should be made after consultation with the appropriate physician, lawyer, or ethics committee member, respectively. Every effort was made to ensure the information in this book was accurate at the time of publication. However, due to this rapidly changing field, the reader is encouraged to consult additional, as well as more recent, sources of information.

Dedication

This book is dedicated to my father, **Dr. Roland F. Wear, Jr.**, the quintessential "doctor's doctor" – a remarkable clinician and teacher. No physician has better mastered the balancing of the art and science of medicine. I was blessed to have such a role model, witnessing both the compassion (in the tone of his voice when talking on the phone with a patient or family member at night) and the passion for the science (during dinner-time discussions). It is only as a physician, that I have come to understand how few truly achieve this balance, and the synergy it creates. It is also in the changing clinical environment of the 90's and 00's that I have gained anew a profound respect for his skill and dedication.

A very special thanks to my loving husband Tom, cherished son Kyle, and dear mother for their total and unconditional love and support.

Acknowledgements

• Dr. David Robinson, a talented physician, educator, and author from "north of the border," for encouraging me to write this book,

• Dr. Harold Bursztajn for his uncommon mentoring,

• Brian Chapman for the excellent illustrations.

Their faith in my ability to accomplish this task made it seem almost easy. . . .sort of. . . .

Rapid Psychler Press

produces books and presentation media that are:

• comprehensively researched

• well organized

• formatted for ease of use

• reasonably priced

• clinically oriented, and

• include humor that enhances education, and that neither demeans patients nor the efforts of those who treat them

Table of Contents

4. Doctor-Patient Relationships/Clinical Issues
54

10. Odds & Ends   206

Author's Foreword

This book is written for anyone with an interest in learning about the major legal issues that practicing physicians face today. Although this text is written primarily for medical doctors, it will be of benefit to the wide range of other professionals who interact with physicians and share many of their responsibilities.

It is little wonder that physicians approach medicolegal issues with distaste, and have not made mastery of these issues a high priority. Physicians have become angry about being told how to practice medicine, and have come to resent many of the requirements for certain actions and detailed documentation. And, like the normal response to things that people resent – we have passively (and at times actively) resisted adopting such requirements.

This is the unfortunate part – many physicians have thrown the proverbial baby out with the bath water where medicolegal issues are concerned. Every mention of limiting liability is seen as a *negative* that has been imposed, rather than studying it and discovering that in these same recommended actions, there is movement towards increasing the autonomy of all involved. Physicians strongly defend their autonomy in practice decisions. Such battles are complimentary to the struggles of our patients, not at odds with them. Helping others to reframe these struggles in several ways and ease the process is one of the goals of this book.

Even if after reading this book you don't have a major philosophical transformation on how you view current practice requirements and behaviors, at least just *consider* that some of these things we are now required to do may be just the right thing to do for the patient.

You may already fall into one of the following categories:

1. Those already knowledgeable about the important medicolegal issues and risk management principles in your practice. Great! This text may fill in the few gaps, update your knowledge, and validate your perceptions.

2. You have been too busy in a residency program or establishing

your practice (with all of the administrative requirements), and are struggling too much with managed care issues to have the time to learn additional information.

3. You have the tendency to practice "defensive medicine" because of your fears of malpractice litigation. Hopefully, the information in this book will give you a better and simpler way to view things. Additionally, you may be able to put your malpractice fears into their proper context.

4. You tend either toward complacency ("It won't happen to me") or worse, a touch of arrogance (I know – it is hard to believe this trait might be present in a physician).

Why read another book to help you minimize your liability? While lecturing to physician groups, I sought out and read almost all of the available texts. Although there are a many excellent books, most are written by psychiatrists, which focus on mental health issues. While applicable to other specialties, these texts may lose the medical student or general practitioner because the focus is so specific. Books with more of a general medical focus books are often written by lawyers and risk managers, not by practicing physicians. Although some of these texts are quite well written, they do not provide a simple "soup to nuts" overview.

What gives me the credibility for this undertaking? Only that I have been each of the proverbial nine blind men with the elephant in the parable (in this case, the hairy managed care medical malpractice mammoth). As an internist in the late 1970's and 80's, I practiced what I thought was good medicine, but now know was often laced with paternalism. In the mid 1980's, I completed a second residency in psychiatry, and discovered what "patient rights" entailed. Attending night school in Washington D.C., in the midst of healthcare reform in the early 1990's, taught me firsthand the issues of healthcare ethics, law, and policy. As the chief operating officer of a clinic, I was responsible for other doctors' practices, policy institution, outside regulations, etc. In this way, I learned about all the external goblins that can act on the delivery of health care. I then returned to a clinical and teaching environment and was able to apply the above lessons – *many of them learned the hard way.*

Why bother learning the issues covered in this book? In addition to improving your mastery of information that strongly affects your practice, you can support what Epstein (1999) termed "mindful practice." He characterizes the important process of ongoing critical self-assessment in the lifelong development of every clinician, and that the best are always reviewing their skills and practice approach on many levels. *"One might postulate that a position of mindlessness is the very thing that gets some clinicians in trouble when it comes to the medicolegal and ethical issues that confront us each and every day."* This book is also a pragmatic risk management exercise. Each item presented here has some risk management value, which helps you to look for ways to limit your liability.

The tone of this book is conversational, not pedantic. While not strictly academic in style, every attempt has been made to provide up-to-date, well-researched, and accurate information. The humor in this book is intended to augment the information, not to demean it, or those to whom it applies. Many clinicians believe that humor has a significant role in the practice of medicine when judiciously shared with our patients (never directed at them). By taking your life's work very seriously, but yourself less so, this book will not seem threatening.

My seven-year-old son recently made a comment to our neighbor that applies to medicolegal risk management. Upon encountering a very large cockroach (fondly known as a palmetto bug in the Florida panhandle), she hesitated, not knowing how to rid herself of it. My son looked at her and said, "Lady, some day you're just going to have to face your fears." The fear of litigation, like the cockroach, is best addressed head on, rather than waiting and hoping that it temporarily scurries away under the bureau.

Finally, a disclaimer – I'm not a lawyer and never will be (thank goodness). Although the information provided here has been thoroughly researched and reviewed, *please do not take it as legal advice*, merely as information. Select a lawyer to advise you on practice issues as carefully as you would the neurosurgeon operating on your aneurysm.

D.J.W-F.
March, 2000

Reference
Epstein, RM: **Mindful Practice**. *JAMA* 282: 833-839, 1999

1. Introduction

There has been an astronomical increase in the number of all types of lawsuits since the 1960's – 70's. Why the increase?

Although many believe it is due to an oversupply of lawyers who are looking for more things to litigate, this may not actually be the case (though perhaps there are exceptions). How this crisis developed, and the relationship between ethical and legal issues requires further exploration.

In a recent survey of physicians, 58% reported that they have been sued at least once. The specialty with the highest percentage of lawsuits was Obstetrics-Gynecology (OB-GYN) at 83%, while Pediatrics was the lowest at 42%. When you realize that you have about a 50:50 chance of being named in a malpractice suit, you can begin to address the issue realistically instead of hoping that it won't happen. The contents of this book offers you the chance to minimize your liability by learning about the most common areas of legal focus – and the particular blind spots in your practice.

As presented in Chapter 2, medical malpractice suits prior to 1960 were based on fairly obvious and egregious cases – as were most non-medical suits, such as employment issues or product liability. The principles of tort law (boring as they may be) are also explained in Chapter 2. An introduction to risk management is presented in Chapter 3. Chapter 4 outlines major issues that clinicians face daily in their interactions with patients. More esoteric (but not less important) issues regarding liability are discussed in Chapter 5.

Following this, there are chapters on managed care, regulatory issues, organizational issues, and specialty-specific information. The text then finishes with some specific tools which describe how to deal with certain high-risk patient scenarios.

Although the chapter on regulatory issues is presented in Chapter 7, this is an area that has given physicians the most concern over the past several years. It has taken on a huge specter of importance – almost overshadowing the medical malpractice concerns.

The Relationship Between Ethics and Law

Ethics are the *principles* of proper or morally correct conduct within a society (a branch of philosophy). **Law** defines the *rules* of conduct as established by a society.

The relationship between ethics and law generally applies in the following way: basic ethical principles frequently lead to the development of law through case precedent and statute. The relationship between the two is dynamic – and based on many forces in society, the nation, and the world.

First, a focus develops on an issue within a society. If enough people feel strongly about the moral "rightness" of the subject, a significant power base develops and legislation may follow. In this way, legislation now formalizes the rules governing certain behaviors.

Even laws are not sufficient to bind individuals to abide by ethical principles. Some regulatory bodies set their standards at an ethical, as opposed to legal, level. Those to whom the regulations apply must then follow the stated standards. An example of this principle involves state boards of medicine. These boards, after full and fair hearings, may suspend or revoke the licenses of physicians, even if a law hasn't been broken. In other instances, court decisions set precedents based on the ethical issues involved in the dispute. Some of the more common non-medical issues involve: abortion rights, capital punishment, and civil commitment.

There is no doubt that the majority of physicians are unequivocally committed to the ethical practice of medicine. Medical ethics focuses on doing what is considered morally right in the evaluation and treatment of patients.

History of Medical Ethics

Medical ethics has a long history, beginning with the Oath of Hippocrates, which is really just a concise statement of principles. The Oath was created during the period of Greek prosperity around the 5th Century BC. Although adapted in the 10th or 11th Century AD to eliminate references to paganism, it has remained as the essential statement of ideal conduct for physicians, and the ideal in protecting patients' rights. The two primary principles of medical ethics are:

Autonomy – the right of every competent person to be able to decide what will be medically done to him or her.

Beneficence – known simply as "do good for the patient" (also known as **nonmalfeasance** – *Do No Harm*).

Thomas Percival, an English physician, made a significant contribution to Western medical ethics with the publication of his Code of Medical Ethics in 1803. In 1847, the first official meeting of the **American Medical Association (AMA)** was held. At that meeting, the founding members adopted the first

American Code of Ethics, which was based on Percival's code. Although there have been revisions, the essence of this code has been maintained. In 1977, a revision was made that sought to achieve a proper and reasonable balance between professional standards and contemporary legal standards.

The preamble from the **1999 AMA Code of Medical Ethics** states that: *"The medical profession has long subscribed to a body of ethical statements developed primarily for the benefit of the patient. As a member of this profession, a physician must recognize responsibility not only to patients, but also to society, to other health professionals, and to self."* The following seven principles adopted by the AMA are not laws, but standards of conduct, which define honorable behavior for physicians.

1. A physician shall be dedicated to providing competent medical service with compassion and respect for human dignity.

2. A physician shall deal honestly with patients and colleagues, and strive to expose those physicians deficient in character or competence, or who engage in fraud or deception.

3. A physician shall respect the law, and also recognize a responsibility to seek changes in those requirements, which are contrary to the best interests of the patient.

4. A physician shall respect the rights of patients, of colleagues, and of other health professionals, and shall safeguard patient confidences within the constraints of the law.

5. A physician shall continue to study, apply, and advance scientific knowledge, make relevant information available to patients, colleagues, and the public, obtain consultation, and use the talents of other health professionals when indicated.

6. A physician shall, in the provision of appropriate patient care, except in emergencies, be free to choose whom to serve, with

whom to associate, and the environment in which to provide medical services.

7. A physician shall recognize a responsibility to participate in activities contributing to an improved community.

In many medical negligence cases or in complaints before state medical boards, lawyers often quote the above principles where there is no statute or case law that is clearly applicable. The full text of the Code of Medical Ethics is published by the Council of Ethical and Judicial Affairs of the AMA. All physicians should have access to this volume, as it addresses clinical issues that occur frequently, as well as others that are less common (e.g. the use of minors as organ donors). It offers references for both peer-reviewed research articles and case law on a wide variety of clinically relevant topics.

The relationship between law and ethics can be further clarified. Ethical values and legal principles are often closely related, *but ethical obligations typically exceed legal duties*. Being cleared of any legal wrongdoing does not necessarily clear one of charges of unethical conduct within a professional society or board of medicine.

Physicians who belong to one or more national medical groups are sent statements of ethics developed by such specialty or subspecialty societies. Membership to these organizations indicates a commitment to the ethical principles so espoused. If a member is charged with violating an ethical principle, the appropriate committee within the organization conducts an investigation. If the charge is found to be valid, the member may be sanctioned or expelled. When this occurs, it may be publicized, and the action sent to that member's state of licensure. It therefore behooves you to be aware of the stated ethical principles of the societies to which you belong.

The Parallel Between Medical Malpractice Litigation and Social Issues

Thirty years ago, you would not have been able to find much written about many of the legal issues which presently affect medical care. Changes have occurred primarily because many of the issues currently considered to be in the legal realm were previously viewed as ethical concerns. While many physicians have the perception that the medical malpractice litigation frenzy of the 1970's, 80's and 90's developed *de novo* (as lawyers discovered new and fertile ground), the roots are much deeper, and not limited to the medical arena.

The changes occurring in the realm of medical malpractice litigation parallel other social issues and their sequelae. From the 1950's – 70's, this country saw many far-reaching changes occurring concurrently: the Civil Rights Movement, Vietnam protests, the Women's Movement, consumers' rights groups, etc. These organizations became very vocal, and very powerful. As support increased for these causes (and the underlying rights they espoused), supportive and protective legislation was passed, and legal precedents were set.

With the passing of enhanced legislation to protect a variety of individual rights, an increase in litigation followed. Lawsuits were brought forth both by individuals and organizations. Many physicians will actively defend their freedom to practice independently. It is the same principle – exercising decision-making autonomy – that has given rise to many of the legal changes in medicine.

Caveat
The autonomy of the physician is *never* lessened by ensuring the autonomy of the patient.

The Scope of Medical Malpractice Litigation

The scope and extent of medical malpractice litigation is quite broad. . . but it could be much worse. Some basic information and factoids to consider are:

A. Between 1977–1992 there were 12,829 physicians involved in 8,231 closed claims:

- Physician care was defensible in 62% of cases and indefensible in 25% (the remainder were indeterminate)
- The plaintiff received payment in 43% of the overall number of claims; patients still received money in 21% of cases where medical care could be defended, but did not always receive money (91%) in cases where medical care could not be defended

- The severity of the injury was not associated with the payment rate in cases resolved by a jury. Other studies have revealed that the severity of the disability predicts an award for the plaintiff (not simply that an adverse event occurred, or that there was negligence involved)

B. In an annual report to Congress in 1991, the Physician Payment Review Commission noted that awards were higher (using identical juries) when it seemed that the defendant could pay more. Jury awards for leg amputation cases (in various scenarios) were:

- $199,999 – auto accident case
- $330,000 – private property owner case
- $687,000 – product liability case
- $754,000 – medical malpractice against a physician
- $761,000 – workman's compensation

C. There has been a definite, and continued increase in the amount of money awarded in medical malpractice cases. For example, from 1995 to 1998 in North Florida:

- The size of the *average* plaintiff verdict has increased from $1.2 million (1995) to $2.6 million (1998)

- The size of the *median* award rose from $270,000 to $665,000

- This compares (favorably?!) with the 1998 *average* award in New York City of $6.1 million, and a *median* of $1.1 million!

(Author's Note: Sincere apologies to those researchers who have provided data from good and valid research. When addressing medical malpractice, there is a huge body of contradictory data, which is why I prefer to call them "factoids" in this presentation.)

Now to the "glass is half full" way of looking at other factoids. There have been several excellent studies looking at hospital admissions and outcomes over time from the 1970's through the '90's. One very consistent fact is that:

- 1% of all hospital records reveal that an injury was caused due to negligence, yet less than 10% of these injuries ever lead to a formal claim.

More factoids:

- Less than 10% of all lawsuits go to juries, and of these, two-thirds find for the defendant physicians (even when physician peer-reviewers found the cases indefensible half of the time!)

- Approximately 4% of all hospitalizations result in adverse events, and more than one-quarter of these are due to substandard care

- There is a 12-fold variation in the rates of adverse events between facilities and physicians; the percentage due to negligence ranges from 0 to 70%

- It is estimated that there are approximately 180,000 deaths annually which can be attributed to iatrogenic causes; half of these are due to negligence

The obvious conclusion to draw is that rather than bemoaning the severity of the medical malpractice crisis – rejoice! It could be much worse. What we as physicians should be most concerned about is minimizing the variation in practice, the incidence of avoidable adverse events, and in particular, the numbers of injuries and deaths due to negligence.

Tort Reform

This may be putting the cart before the horse (the discussion of torts is in the next chapter), but it is important to see the big picture of litigation, and be aware of the competing forces involved in determining the amount of money at stake in litigation.

As the settlements awarded by juries increased, so did malpractice insurance costs. Multiple steps were taken to curb the skyrocketing costs, and tort reform was one of these measures. Many states have enacted legislation that limits the amount of money a jury can award to a plaintiff in medical malpractice cases (and other civil cases). Sixteen states have laws that limit the amount of recovery for non-economic damages (including pain and suffering, inconvenience, disfigurement, loss of quality of life, etc.). Five other states have a limit on economic damages (discussed in Chapter 2). Some states do not allow awards for non-economic damages (such as pain and suffering). There are also a variety of requirements for arbitration, settlement conferences, and other options designed to avert a jury trial (and decrease the astronomical costs of litigation).

An example of early tort reform (established in 1975) is in the state of California, that has a $250,000 cap on the amount a person can receive to compensate for pain and suffering.

Other mechanisms focus on attorneys' fees, and may limit the percentage an attorney can collect on **contingency** (which means the lawyer does not get paid unless he or she wins). The attention to fees is an attempt to limit the incentive for an attorney to pursue cases – i.e. he may not take a case if he'll win only $250,000, but is far more likely to if he thinks he can win several million dollars.

In spite of all the negative information you hear, remember that only 10% of cases ever get to a jury trial, and of that 10%, about two-thirds of juries find for the defendant physician(s).

Why Do Patients Sue?

Before launching into an overview of negligence law (followed by the many situations that place you at risk for experiencing a suit), consider this simple equation:

Medical Malpractice Suit = Bad Outcome + Bad Feelings

A bad outcome is just that – there *must* be some tangible physical or psychological injury. Although a patient may not like a physician's looks or attitude, or not improve from the treatment provided, these are not adequate grounds for a lawsuit. There must be an actual *injury* (more to follow).

We all have known, seen, or heard of physicians who were not the best in the skill department (e.g. "I wouldn't let Dr. Nincompoop take care of my dog. . .") and he would at times have a bad outcome. Yet, the patients never seemed to sue him. Why? Because they liked him. He probably has a great bedside manner and demonstrates genuine concern. This may have been accomplished through active listening and facial expressions/demeanor indicating empathy. As far as the patient was concerned, the doctor could do no wrong (which emphasizes the importance of peer review in some cases!).

At the other end of the spectrum, we have some colleagues of whom you might joke, "I would never see Dr. I.M. Godsgift unless I was *really* sick." These are the folks who may be brilliant in their respective fields, but have almost reptilian personalities. They usually don't see this as a problem, or may be so arrogant they don't care – but the patients (or their families) do. As you'll see, the recurrent theme of effective communication will become evident. Talking to a person using polysyllabic jargon in a condescending manner does not constitute effective communication. The resentment that most people feel when they are spoken down to may not become evident if all goes well. However, when there is a problem, all of this resentment comes bubbling to the surface and finds somewhere to vent (like a bad remake of *The Poltergeist*).

Many authors report a quasi-rule of thirds:

- One-third of patients will never sue
- One-third will sue if they ever get a chance
- The rest fall somewhere between

Beware of the latter group, and don't give them a reason to want to seek out an attorney with your name on their minds, lips, or subpoenas.

One survey found that 98% of patients wanted or expected their doctor to acknowledge an error whether this caused any harm or not (more on this in the last chapter). The patients who suffered from moderate to severe errors were more likely to report the doctor to authorities or consider suing if the doctor failed to disclose the error. Most people do not expect their doctors to be perfect, but they do expect them to be honest.

A study of families who sued their child's doctor after a perinatal injury showed that 24% of those who filed a lawsuit did so when they realized the physician:

- Was not completely honest
- Allowed them to believe things that were not true
- Intentionally mislead them

Another 20% sued because they said it was the only way they could find out what really happened!

One unsettling editorial by a physician spoke of his recommendation to a friend that he sue his surgeon after an operation was performed removing all but the upper 5% of his stomach (because of a misdiagnosis of gastric cancer). It turned out to be peptic ulcer disease. What angered the patient (and his physician friend) was the flippant response of the surgeon who offered neither an explanation nor an apology.

References

American Medical Association: **Code of Medical Ethics – Current Opinions with Annotations**.
American Medical Association, Chicago, 1999

Borbjerg RR: **Medical Malpractice and Folklore, Facts, and the Future**.
Annals of Int Med 117:788-791, 1992

Bozeman FC: **Sky-High South Florida Verdicts Spread to North Florida**.
Escambia County Medical Society Bulletin, Oct 1999

Brennan T: **The Harvard Medical Practice Study**.
The Mental Health Practitioner and the Law.
Harvard University Press, Cambridge, 1998

Brennan TA, Sox CM, Burstin HR: **Relation Between Negligent Adverse Events in the Outcomes of Medical Malpractice Litigation**.
N Engl J Med 335:1963-1967, 1996

Crane M: **Malpractice Wars**.
Medical Economics 26, July 1999

Hickson GB, Clayton EW, Githens PB, et al: **Factors That Prompted Families to File Medical Malpractice Claims Following Perinatal Injuries**.
JAMA 267:1359-1363, 1992

Lally JJ: **Why I Urged My Friend to Sue His Doctors**.
Medical Economics 151-152, July 26, 1999

Sloan FA: **Medical Malpractice Experience of Physicians: Predictable Or Haphazard?**
JAMA 262:3291, 1989

Taragin MI, Willett LR, Wilcek AP et al: **The Influence of Standard Of Care and Severity of Injury on the Resolution of Medical Malpractice Claims**.
Annals of Int Med 117:780-784, 1992

Tort Reform Battles: Sometimes the Force Is With You.
Medical Economics, 133-142, July 26, 1999

Vidmar N: *Medical Malpractice and the American Jury*.
University of Michigan Press, Ann Arbor, 1997

Witman AB, Park DM, Hardin SB: **How Do Patients Want Physicians to Handle Mistakes?**
Arch Intern Med 156:2565-2569, 1996

2. Legal Stuff

Before providing a brief overview of medical malpractice law, it is important to understand the bigger picture of the legal system in the United States.

Criminal and Civil Law

There are two basic types of law in the U.S. – criminal and civil. The basis of U.S. law is derived from our Constitution and from English common law. The goal of **criminal law** is to effect justice and to dispense punishment for crimes committed. The aim of **civil law** is to make restitution to the wronged party, or "to make whole again." The roots of this tradition go back to the Talmud. Today, the "making whole" usually has to do with $$$.

Sources of Law
The United States Constitution
This established the U.S. as a republic and provided the structure of our system of congress. It is the gold standard by which all other laws applied to Americans are judged. In addition to the Articles, it also includes the Bill of Rights.

Bill of Rights
This further defines the individual rights of all Americans (interestingly, several states would not ratify the Constitution without a guarantee that individual rights would be protected through this provision). Some of these rights are: freedom of speech, freedom of the press, freedom of religion, freedom to assemble and protest, protection against unreasonable searches and seizures of property, protection against cruel and unusual punishment, etc. The majority of the 16 additional amendments expand individual rights and freedoms.

State Constitutions
Every state has its own constitution and laws. The only guiding principle is that state laws cannot conflict with federal law. They can be more comprehensive in the protection of individual rights than federal laws, but not less so. For example, federal law amended the **standard of proof** for civil commitment to be that of "clear and convincing evidence." States with lesser standards (i.e. preponderance of evidence), were then required to adopt the federal standard. States already requiring a higher standard (i.e. beyond a reasonable doubt) were free to keep this standard. The goal of this implementation was to protect every individual's right to freedom, and to err in the direction of allowing liberty. For example, individual states are allowed to grant greater protection to individuals against involuntary hospitalization than the federal standard, but not less.

Statutes
Statutes are laws adopted by elected state and local officials,

and by the U.S. Congress. Some of the statutes that are important for healthcare are the **Occupational Safety and Health Act (OSHA)**, **Americans with Disabilities Act (ADA)**, **Civil Rights Act (CRA)**, **False Claims Act (FCA)**, and the **Food and Drug Act**.

Regulatory or Administrative Law

For many, the regulations set by numerous local, state, and federal agencies have a more pervasive impact on daily life than many of the more prominent sources listed above. Examples of administrative agencies that affect healthcare workers are: **Health Care Financing Administration (HCFA)**, **Occupational Safety and Health Administration (OSHA)**, **Food and Drug Administration (FDA)**, **Equal Employment Opportunity Commission (EEOC)**, and the **National Labor Relations Board (NLRB)**. For healthcare professionals requiring licensure, state licensing boards are also very powerful regulatory agencies.

Common Law

This source of law dates back to 12th century England. When there were no legal precedents to assist judges with their legal decisions, they applied current customs and their own common sense to come to decisions.

Case Law

This is also known as "judge-made law." Case law develops when judges interpret and apply sources of law in particular cases. A decision so rendered then sets a precedent for future cases in that jurisdiction, as well as in similar and lower courts. Decisions made by the U.S. Supreme Court provide precedent for all other similar cases in the U.S. The concept of **stare decisis** (Latin for, "let the decision stand") means that controlling case law can only be modified by a higher-level court. Only the Supreme Court can modify one of its own decisions (this rarely happens). Medical negligence cases are almost always determined by case law.

Medical Malpractice Law/Torts 101

Knowledge is indeed power. Here, knowledge of the rules of malpractice lawsuits helps to demystify them and decrease the accompanying anxiety. As any first year law student will tell you, one of the most boring, yet crucially important courses is *Introduction to Tort Law*. Many doctors feel a sense of relief after learning the basics of medical negligence law. They realize that their fears are often worse than reality.

A **tort** is any civil wrong against another person. Tort law covers civil actions between two parties, which are defined as either *intentional* or *unintentional torts*.

Intentional torts are deliberate actions which may cause damage. They are not usually covered by malpractice insurance. Examples include: assault and battery, sexual relationships with patients, and false imprisonment.

Unintentional torts are actions that possess an unreasonable risk of causing harm. Medical malpractice falls under this broader area of negligence law.

The Four Arms of Any Negligence Case
The 4 D'S
There are four components required for a negligence action to be considered valid. These are called the four D's of negligence (similar to the four F's of gallbladder disease!). The four D's that a plaintiff must establish for a successful negligence suit are:

- **Duty** (of a doctor to a patient)
- **Dereliction** of duty, or a deviation from the standard of care
- **Direct Causation** of the problem
- **Damage** (an injury was caused)

For a negligence suit to be considered (or as the lawyers say "have merit"), some form of injury (physical or emotional) must be present. If not, a lawsuit cannot be launched, even if a physician has blatantly violated accepted standards of care. On the other hand, an unfavorable outcome for one of your patients does not mean you will automatically be sued. Depending on your specialty and the acuity level of your patients, there is the ever-present risk of unfavorable outcomes. When they occur, it does not reflect on you as a physician – uncertainty is an integral part of medical practice. Neurosurgeons, for example, understand that a large percentage of their patients are expected to fare poorly. Psychiatrists, at some point during their careers, can expect at least one patient to commit suicide.

First, a duty must be established. A **duty** to a patient begins any time there is a **doctor-patient relationship (DPR)**. When a DPR is established, the doctor has a duty to provide a certain **standard of care (SOC)** for that patient.

If there is evidence that the SOC is breached, a dereliction of the duty is considered to have occurred, which is the next link necessary in a successful malpractice action. The final step involves demonstrating that the dereliction (or deviation from the SOC) was the direct causation of the patient's injury.

Standard of Proof

Each of the four elements in alleged negligence cases must be proven to a specific legal standard. If you have ever testified as an expert witness or read a case transcript, you will be familiar with the following statement made by expert witnesses, "I can state with reasonable medical certainty that. . ."

The legal standard of proof required in negligence cases in almost all jurisdictions is called a **preponderance of evidence**. This is considered to be "more likely than not" or, for those who think numerically, is at least 51% certain. With very few exceptions, the plaintiff in a malpractice claim must show, with a *preponderance of evidence*, that the alleged negligence was indeed the defendant's responsibility. The majority of civil cases use preponderance of evidence as the legal standard.

Other legal standards exist. The next highest standard of proof is called that of **clear and convincing evidence**. This is used in civil cases where there is a more substantial right at risk (rather than mere monetary remuneration), such as someone's liberty (as in a civil commitment), or the right of a hospitalized psychiatric patient to refuse medication. The clear and convincing standard is considered to be somewhere in the vicinity of 75 – 85% certainty.

The highest standard of proof is called **beyond a reasonable doubt**, and is considered to be about 95% certainty. This standard is applied in criminal cases and in some jurisdictions for specific civil actions. To believe something beyond a reasonable doubt means "you better be darn sure!"

More About the Four D's

Duty

Duty to a patient is established by formally providing medical services (such as assignment to your primary care panel or in a consultation). It can also be implied, as in working in an emergency room (ER) and treating patients seeking care there.

Situations that are less clear might involve a neighbor requesting your medical advice. The law presumes that when a physician provides some form of evaluation/treatment, even informally, a duty to that person has been established. You may want to rethink the "cocktail party consult" the next time you are asked for your advice – or at least be very circumspect in your comments. It is safe to say something like "That's a good question – I think you should contact your doctor about this matter as it is not really appropriate for me to give you advice."

Once a DPR has been is established, the physician has the duty to provide the SOC for that patient.

Direct Causation

Determining cause in malpractice cases generally involves two factors:

- **Cause-in-fact**, which refers to whether "but for" the alleged act, the injury would not have occurred

- **Proximate cause**, which is a substantial factor in the resultant injury; this also is related to the term of *foreseeability*

Legal and medical perspectives differ on how an action is seen as the direct cause of an injury. In medicine, we are used to diagnosing a disease and determining the causative agent, which (frequently) becomes the focus of treatment. From a legal standpoint, direct or proximate cause is determined by looking at whether the action *foreseeably* could have caused the injury, and whether the injury would not have occurred "but for" the actions of the physician.

Damage

Any successful medical malpractice lawsuit must contain evidence that there was some type of injury sustained. Such "damage" is usually a compensable injury or a death that occurs because of a specific act or omission. The most common types of acts or omissions include:

- Incorrect diagnosis
- Delays in making a diagnosis or instituting treatment
- Providing inappropriate treatment
- Medication side-effects or errors
- Procedural errors

The type of compensation the plaintiff seeks is referred to as **damages** (not to be confused with injury) of which there are three types:

- Economic
- Non-economic
- Punitive

Economic damages are those costs that are directly associated to the injury. These can include medical bills, lost wages, and loss of earning potential.

Non-economic damages are also known as **compensatory damages**, and are moneys given for things like "pain and suffering," "loss of consortium" with a spouse, or "lost quality of life." Some jurisdictions do not allow compensation for non-economic damages without a physical or psychological injury, and some do not allow non-economic damages at all. Many states also have **caps** (a ceiling) on the total amount that can be collected for these types of damages.

The last category of damages is called **punitive**, referring to damages awarded to the plaintiff(s) to punish the defendant. When punitive damages are awarded, the cases usually involve very clear acts of negligence. Punitive damages are rare against physicians; they are much more likely to be sought in lawsuits against organizations, drug companies, etc.

An example of punitive damages involved the General Motors Corporation. In this action, economic and non-economic damages totaling $107.6 million dollars were awarded to the plaintiffs, who had experienced severe burns when their vehicles burst into flames after being rear-ended. There was an additional *$48 billion dollars* awarded in punitive damages. This case was seen as being particularly egregious by the jury because clear documentation was provided that GM management decided not to recall the automobiles with the problem (once they were aware of it), because it would cost more to fix the problem than it would to defend a lawsuit. This blatant disregard for consumer safety clearly didn't sit well with the jury.

Examples of punitive damages in the healthcare arena can be found in recent lawsuits against two large managed care organizations. The first case involves the 1998 multimillion-dollar Kentucky jury award against Humana, Inc. Here, economic damages were limited to the payment of medical bills. The remainder of the award was given for punitive damages. This case was followed by the January, 1999 verdict of $116 million against Aetna Healthplans of California for punitive damages.

Standard of Care

The **standard of care (SOC)** is generally defined as practicing with the same reasonable level of skill that a prudent physician with similar training and experience would recognize as adequate and acceptable in similar circumstances. Readers are encouraged to check with your state medical practice statute for the exact definition.

With few exceptions, the SOC is based on national standards, not local ones. The definition of SOC does not necessarily specify the best, most expensive, or technologically advanced care that can be provided. Rather, it refers to care that is considered "acceptable" and "adequate" to similarly trained practitioners working under similar circumstances.

How Do I Measure SOC?

This is indeed the million-dollar question (pun intended). It would be great if there were absolute parameters in each case of alleged medical negligence, but this isn't so. Most definitions contain vague terms like "acceptable" and "reasonable."

Because the SOC is based on the care that a similarly trained doctor would provide, most state laws clearly indicate that not just any physician can testify as an expert witness. If the charges are against a non-residency trained general practitioner, then the doctor presenting testimony will have similar training and experience. If the alleged malpractice involves a board-certified neurosurgeon, an obstetrician will not be called to testify. The SOC is a national standard. It doesn't vary for medicine practiced in the backwoods or in a state-of-the-art facility.

The reason that the majority of areas have abandoned local standards primarily is that it may be impossible to get one physician to testify against another who practices in the same area. Secondly, with the improvements in communication over the past decades, it is reasonable to hold physicians accountable to a national level.

The SOC is derived from many sources, including the **Joint Commission for the Accreditation of Healthcare Organizations (JCAHO)** standards, specialty guidelines, local facility policies, etc. The SOC evolves over time, and the courts look to medical personnel for guidance on these issues. This is the reason that most jurisdictions require that an expert witness in a medical malpractice case have training and experience similar to the defendant.

An example of an evolving SOC is the use of beta-blockers at the time of discharge following a myocardial infarction (MI). In the early 1990's, it became evident that there was significantly less morbidity and mortality in patients who were treated with beta-blockers after an MI. The American Heart Association recommended this treatment be considered for all patients upon discharge from hospital. Over the following several years, the data collected was even more conclusive, and the recommendations were also adopted by general medical journals, including the Journal of the American Medical Association (JAMA). These recommendations were given to general physicians, not just cardiologists. After several studies noted a high rate of underutilization for the post-MI use of beta-blockers, the American Medical Association made a formal recommendation in late 1998. This Quality Care Alert was mailed to every member of the AMA –

If you do not at least consider treatment of your post-MI patients with a beta-blocker (or do not document why you did not treat your post-MI patient with a beta-blocker), and your patient suffers significant morbidity or mortality after discharge from the hospital, an attorney could raise this as evidence that you deviated from the established standard of care, and you might be found negligent if sued. Nowhere does anything state that you must prescribe the beta-blocker, only that you should consider its use.

Further Comments on the SOC

When using medications, be careful if you are prescribing something for a non-FDA approved use. Always state your rationale, which should be supportable by peer review references. Also, the **Physicians Desk Reference (PDR)** has been used as the SOC in several cases when a drug was used in a dosage outside the recommended range, or for a different duration of treatment. You can use a drug in ways that you believe are appropriate as long as you document your reasons.

Another interesting catch is that if the alleged injury is said to be caused by a deviation from the SOC, and the defendant did not follow the guidance in the PDR, the standard of proof may shift to the defense in some jurisdictions. This means that *you* (not the plaintiff) must prove, with a preponderance of the evidence, that you met the SOC instead of the plaintiff needing to prove that you did not. There are many times where it is perfectly appropriate to use a drug for a non-approved use, just be certain to note why, and on what basis. Well-conducted, prospective, double-blind studies are required for medications to receive FDA approval. Such studies are frequently funded by pharmaceutical companies. Two key reasons that a drug company may not be particularly interested in pursuing FDA approval (and committing millions of dollars to research) are:

- Where the group of persons who might benefit from that particular use of the drug would be small (which would provide a scant profit)

- When the patent for a particular drug is due to expire in the near future

Alternative Treatments and SOC

A brief introduction is provided here on alternative/ complementary medicine and SOC (more information is contained in Chapter 10). Alternative treatments include therapies ranging from herbal medicines to acupuncture. Rather than a discussion about the efficacy of such treatments, a caution will be given:

If there is evidence that you prescribed an alternative treatment that allegedly led to an injury, you will not be found to meet the SOC if other, reasonably prudent, similarly trained and experienced physicians, would not also consider this treatment in a similar situation.

Caveat

Familiarize yourself with all the policies that your organization has in place, as well as the guidelines your practice has developed. All local policies will be used as legal evidence of the SOC under which you should be practicing. Policies should state the minimum standards required by law (and not set a higher standard).

The same goes for JCAHO/**National Committee of Quality Assurance (NCQA)** standards. Even if your organization is not required to be certified by either agency, meeting the basic standards set by these organizations is a good idea, and demonstrates a commitment to providing a certain level of quality care. If you practice in a JCAHO or NCQA accredited institution, these standards will be considered to be the SOC for your organization.

Medical Malpractice Litigation Process

There are many steps involved in a medical malpractice lawsuit. This actual process varies from state to state. An example of the preliminary process (prior to the actual trial) in Florida is as follows:

1. A dissatisfied patient/family speaks with a lawyer to discuss legal action. The idea for a lawsuit may have come from speaking with family or friends, a decision following a period of personal reflection, or after mounting frustration over the lack of answers after a bad outcome.

2. The plaintiff's lawyer must perform a pre-suit investigation of all factors. Written corroboration from a medical expert witness stating that there are reasonable grounds to support the claim of negligence is necessary.

3. At this point, the plaintiff's lawyer can provide a notice of intent to submit a claim against the defendants listed (in the "deep pockets" theory of litigation, all potential parties will be named, as explained on page 32).

4. The defense then conducts an investigation to determine if the defendants were negligent in the care or treatment of the claimant to the point of causing an injury. If this is not found to be the case, such a finding requires a written expert statement from a physician who has training and experience similar to that of the defendant.

5. Following the pre-suit investigation, any party can file a motion to request that the court (judge) determine if pursuing the claim is reasonable or not.

6. The parties may elect to have damages awarded by arbitration, which is one of two forms of **alternative dispute resolution (ADR)**. Mediation is the other. Punitive damages cannot be awarded in ADR.

7. Upon receipt of a claim, the prospective defendant(s) can make an offer to admit liability and accept arbitration, which must be made within 50 days. If arbitration is rejected, a lawsuit may be filed within 60 days or before the statute of limitations (see below).

8. If a settlement is accepted, the parties have 30 days to agree on an amount; if this is not achievable, the case goes to binding arbitration.

Although convoluted, this sequence of events provides opportunities for minimizing the number of cases that proceed to trial, while ensuring that individuals are able to receive fair compensation for their injuries.

Two States – Two Sets of Rules

A comparison of Maryland and Florida state laws illustrates the wide variation between jurisdictions. The following table highlights four important elements involved in a malpractice suit, which are:

- **Statute of Limitations**
- **Contributory Negligence**
- **Vicarious Liability**
- **Expert Testimony**

Statute of Limitations (SOL)

SOL is the amount of time a plaintiff has to file a lawsuit following the injury. Different states have different SOLs, and they vary considerably. The SOL can also vary if there is evidence of fraud or an attempt to conceal mistakes; the period of time a plaintiff has to initiate a claim may be extended in such cases. If the family is suing for a wrongful death action (as a result of malpractice) a different set of rules apply.

Contributory Negligence

Contributory negligence is the consideration as to whether the plaintiff contributed to the injury which is the focus of the lawsuit. This frequently becomes an issue when a patient is noncompliant with treatment or does not take even minimal responsibility for maintaining a healthy life style.

	Florida	Maryland
Statute of Limitations	2 years from the date the incident occurred or should have been discovered, up to a maximum of 4 years from the time of the injury, unless the patient is a child under the age of 8 years.	5 years from the time of the injury, or 3 years from when it was discovered. This applies to patients older than the age of 11 years.
If fraud is alleged	Maximum of 7 years, or if the patient is a child, age 11 years.	
In wrongful death suits	2 years from the time of death.	3 years from the time of death.
Contributory Negligence	The award is decreased in proportion to the degree of negligence. Even if there is a large amount of contributory negligence, this does not bar the plaintiff from receiving an award.	Any negligence by the plaintiff bars recovery (Maryland is one of the very few states with this statute).
Vicarious Liability	May be allowed if there is an apparent agency.	Same as Florida.
Expert Testimony	The notice of intent must have a medical expert's opinion stating that there is grounds for negligence.	Not required.

Vicarious Liability

This is a consideration of whether any additional person or organization, by virtue of their relationship to the defendant, also has responsibility for injury to the plaintiff (this is also presented below).

Expert Testimony

This may be a required step in filing a lawsuit. Increasingly, affidavits are required at the time of filing (or shortly afterwards) which assert the validity of the allegations made. Again, the expert in most jurisdictions should be a physician with similar training and experience to that of the defendant physician.

Other Issues Related to Legal Matters

RES IPSA LOQUITOR

One exception to having a similarly trained physician testify (and in some states provide an affidavit prior to filing a formal suit) involves cases that fall under the category of **res ipsa loquitor**, which literally translated means "let the thing speak for itself." This is used when the alleged deviation from the SOC is so egregious as to be blatantly obvious to the layperson (i.e. the judge and/or jury, called the **finder of fact** in these cases).

Although there are four elements that must be satisfied legally to have a *res ipsa loquitor* situation (described below), the short form test is the following – if, after you are told the story, you cringe, make a face, and mutter "Oh my Gosh!" – it is a blatant case. Examples are: amputating the wrong leg, operating on the wrong person, leaving various and sundry surgical tools in body cavities, etc.

For those who are gluttons for this stuff, the legal requirements for a *res ipsa loquitor* case are:

- The harm rarely occurs in the absence of negligence (i.e. one doesn't normally cut off the wrong leg in surgery unless there is an obvious problem)

- The situation must have been under the sole control of the defendant physician (e.g. the Operating Room technician cannot be at fault when the surgeon is the only one operating the saw)

- The plaintiff did not contribute to the bad result (she didn't jump up during surgery and point to the wrong leg as the one with the problem)

- Only the defendants have access to information about what happened

Once a case is established as falling under *res ipsa loquitor*, the standard of proof shifts to the defense. Rather than the plaintiff having to prove negligence by the preponderance of evidence, the defense must prove there was no negligence involved.

Vicarious Liability

This term describes the additional liability that a person or organization (other than the defendant) may face in a negligence action.

The reason that vicarious liabilities have taken on such an important role is principally what is known as the "deep pockets" theory of negligence lawsuits. Willie Sutton aptly stated this principle when he was asked why he robbed banks – "Because that's where the money is!" A good lawyer will aim charges of negligence at the deepest pocket available. This is done for the simple reason of obtaining the largest possible settlement. There is the additional psychological advantage of identifying the defendant as a faceless corporation rather than the individual physician. A jury may be hesitant to find an individual (particularly a physician) guilty if the case is "iffy," but is much more likely to find for the plaintiff if a wealthy corporation is the defendant.

Still another reason for an attorney to pursue the largest entity possible involves the potential for punitive damages. A jury would clearly request significantly higher punitive damages from a corporation worth hundreds of millions of dollars than an individual with a much lower net worth. This is a principle seen frequently in product liability cases.

In the "deep pockets" approach to civil litigation, the attorney for the plaintiff will always try to include the organization with the largest financial reserve. Federal and state governments, like other large organizations, are considered to have some of the deepest pockets around. An example of current "deep pockets litigation" involves tobacco companies. No lawsuits have been brought against individuals who may have had a role in "distorting the truth" in these cases. Punitive damages against large managed care corporations follow this same rule.

Frequently the doctor, the hospital staff, the hospital that granted the doctor privileges, the parent organization, etc. will all be named in a lawsuit, with the expectation that some of the above may be dropped as the process proceeds. In a medical negligence suit, any health care provider holding privileges and whose name appears in the medical record is typically mentioned at the outset of the lawsuit. Only those that are found to meet all four of the required arms of a negligence case will actually be named in the final lawsuit.

Two terms you may hear are those of **apparent** or **ostensible agency/authority**. These terms mean that a reasonable person would assume that an organization would in some way be responsible for the defendant's actions (even if they ultimately are not). For example, an organization offering ER services with contracted staff may be found to have vicarious liability if a person being treated in that ER might reasonably believe the staff worked for the organization, rather than the contractor.

RESPONDEAT SUPERIOR

Similar to vicarious liability, **respondeat superior** refers to the principle where a "master" may be held liable for the acts of his "servants" (sound like your residency?). Employers can be held responsible for the negligence of their employees (and are frequently found to be). Thus, doctors may be held liable for the acts of their employees or others under their supervision. Keep this principle in mind if **physician extenders** are employed in your practice. This is also an important consideration when psychiatrists are members of "treatment teams" but are unaware of the supervisory responsibilities for those practicing under their licenses.

This "captain of the ship" doctrine also applies to academic medicine. Staff physicians who work on wards where residents are active providers, and in particular where medical students are also treating patients, are subject to *respondeat superior*. This applies even when the supervision of students is delegated to residents. This is discussed further in Chapter 8.

National Practitioner Data Bank (NPDB)

The 1986 Health Care Quality Improvement Act established the NPDB. It is administered by the Bureau of Health Professions of the Department of Health and Human Services, and began receiving reports in 1990. The NPDB was instituted to prevent doctors with substandard skills from hopping between states. A physician's name is required to be reported to the NPDB when:

- There is *any* award given to the plaintiff as the result of a negligence action (even a settlement with no presumption of guilt, or a $1 finding for the plaintiff)

- Any case of an adverse privileging action

- An action is taken by a state board of medicine against a licensed physician

- An action is taken against a member by a professional medical association

From 1990 – 1996, there were 145,299 reports made:

- 118,211 (81%) were malpractice payments
- 20,707 (14%) were licensure actions
- 5,963 (4%) were privileging actions
- 268 were from professional societies
- 150 actions involved the DEA

Registered nurses and allied health professionals can also be reported.

Clinical Guidelines

For the purpose of this discussion, **clinical guidelines** are any written instruction regarding the appropriate evaluation and/or treatment for a particular disease, diagnosis, or symptom complex. The use of clinical guidelines can reduce the incidence of substandard treatment (and preventable errors), and minimize the use of defensive medicine (with its own risks and costs).

Clinical guidelines are also known by a variety of other terms: **practice parameters**, **treatment pathways**, **medical**

guidelines, and **clinical policies**. Practitioners must be aware of the guidelines that their facility, practice, county, state, specialty association, etc. have established for their scope of practice. If these guidelines are taken in the spirit that they are intended, they can be very helpful. While many physicians resent being told how to practice medicine, guidelines do not impose strict requirements for adherence. Prudent clinicians clearly document their rationale for providing a form of treatment that significantly deviates from established guidelines.

Clinical guidelines are helpful when it comes to providing evidence that the SOC was met. In Maine, as part of a demonstration project, a medical malpractice case is automatically decided in favor of the defendant if it can be established that he adhered to the state-developed guidelines when treating a patient. Of course, the converse can also apply.

Nuisance Lawsuits

Nuisance lawsuits are those that are filed when the plaintiff may accept a "nominal" settlement deemed by the defendant's insurer to be a lower amount than the cost of taking the case to a jury trial (even when the case is defensible). The monetary value of "nominal" or "nuisance" is based on the size or worth of the organization being sued, and may be $50,000 (or more). Physicians may be sued, and despite a lack of evidence showing negligence, may not get their day in court. Insurance companies weigh the cost of proceeding to trial against the amount of the proposed settlement. Their decisions are based on finances, not principles. Most physicians want to have the opportunity to defend their actions and be absolved of all guilt (both for personal reasons and so a report doesn't get sent to the NPDB).

Caveat

Check your professional negligence policy to see if you have waived the right to take an action to court if the insurance company decides to settle.

Intentional Torts

There are two types of torts, **intentional** and **unintentional**. Most doctors are unaware of their risk of being sued for an intentional tort. If at all possible, the plaintiff's lawyer can (and usually will) submit a lawsuit for both types of torts – they are not limited to only one course of action.

An **intentional tort** involves intended, volitional conduct (which can be an action or an omission) by one person, with an increased certainty (or intent) that harm will occur, and which results in injury to another person or her property. The distinction between an *intentional tort* and *negligence* involves:

- The degree of likelihood that something bad will result from the action or omission

- The person's intent

Most negligence actions are not considered to be intentional torts. There are several reasons why someone might initiate a lawsuit for an intentional tort:

- Relative ease of proof: The 4 D's do not need to be proven – all that is required to show culpability for an intentional tort is the action occurred and there was a resultant injury; there is no need for an expert witness in these cases (there is no SOC issue)

- There is a much greater likelihood of the plaintiff receiving punitive damages in an intentional tort because of the forseeability of an injury occurring

- The statute of limitations may not be limited to 2 or 3 years (the norm in most jurisdictions) from the time the patient knew, or should have known of the injury

The main reason that intentional torts (even ones likely to be successful) against physicians are infrequently pursued, is that these actions are not often covered by a physician's malpractice insurance policy. Resulting settlements are likely to be lower than pursuing other types of lawsuits. Although some plaintiffs file complaints "just on principle," the usual goal of a civil suit is to receive as much remuneration as possible. Furthermore, most attorneys do not take cases unless they feel confident they can win, or at least obtain a substantial settlement agreement. A list of common types of intentional torts appears below. Many of these are discussed in other sections of this book:

- Abandonment
- Assault
- Battery
- Breach of Contract
- Defamation
- False imprisonment
- Fraud

- Intentional infliction of emotional distress
- Invasion of privacy
- Libel
- Sexual assault/battery
- Slander

Assault and Battery are discussed in the informed consent section in Chapter 4. Remember that any nonconsensual touching can be considered battery (e.g. performing surgery without proper informed consent). Assault is defined as the threat to cause harm.

Defamation/Libel/Slander/Invasions of Privacy are addressed in the confidentiality violations section in Chapter 4.

Sexual Assault & Battery are presented in the boundary issues section of Chapter 4. An interesting legal strategy can develop when a physician is charged after having sex with a patient. Rather than charge the doctor with sexual battery, he may be charged with "mishandling the transference" (particularly if he is a psychiatrist). This becomes a matter of "medical negligence" instead of an intentional tort, and therefore is covered by malpractice insurance. How creative!

False imprisonment is covered in Chapter 4.

Intentional infliction of emotional distress is interesting, in that *anyone* can use this as a catchall category if they believe "they've been done wrong."

Breach of contract: A contract can be implied, verbal (as in a discussion with a patient), or written. Almost any DPR involves some form of implied contract. The patient agrees to come to you for an evaluation, provide their history, and comply with the agreed course of treatment. Physicians agree to provide quality medical care for patients (at least the SOC), answer their questions, and not abandon them.

Some physicians make the mistake of promising their patients a certain outcome, which occurs in a variety of forms:

- To a patient coming to you for treatment of major depression: *"If you take this medication you will feel much better in a short time."*

- To a patient with obesity: *"If you follow my regimen you will lose all the weight you want."*

- To a patient discussing a bone marrow biopsy: *"It will only hurt a little."*

- To a patient considering augmentation mammoplasty: *"You will be really satisfied and feel a lot more attractive."*

- To the family of an accident victim in the ER: *"We'll do everything possible to save her!"*

Within any specialty, there are many possible analogies to the above examples. The simplest guideline is to *never promise*. Even if you believe what you are promising, there are always some patients who don't read the textbooks!

Remember the "rule of thirds." For a breach of contract suit, all the patient needs to prove is that you promised something that wasn't delivered. A few jurisdictions require a written contract, but in most you can be sued for breach of a verbal contract.

Examples of appropriate (and safe) responses in the above scenarios are:

- The depression patient: *"The majority of patients with symptoms like yours begin to get some relief over the course of several weeks."*

- The obese patient: *"If we work together on your nutritional and exercise regimen, I think you can achieve realistic results."*

- Pending bone marrow biopsy: *"The procedure can be painful, but we will provide several medications to reduce your discomfort, and explain the process to you in detail."*

- Augmentation mammoplasty: *"We can review the probable physical results but we need to also discuss the reasons you desire this procedure, and what your expectations are."*

- The accident victim's family: *"I'm sorry – your family member is in critical condition. We'll do the best we can under the circumstances to save her."*

Caveat

What you don't want to do is paint yourself into the proverbial corner and then be left explaining why the promised outcome didn't occur.

Several organizations have been successfully sued by patients and their families for breach of contract on the basis of not providing what was advertised in their pamphlets. Examples of problematic phrases are as follows:

- "All of our doctors are board certified"

- "Full range of wellness services available"

- "All mental health needs met"

- "Your doctor makes your treatment decisions - not an administrator"

- *You* can choose your doctor"

- "Care available 24 hours per day"

References

American Medical Association:
Beta-blocker Prophylaxis After MI.
Quality Care Alert. AMA, 1998

Archer JD: **The FDA Does Not Approve Uses of Drugs**.
JAMA 252:1054-1055, 1984

Cabana MD, Rand CS, Powe NR et al: **Why Don't Physicians Follow Clinical Practice Guidelines?**
JAMA 282:1458-1465

Garnick DW, Hendricks AM, Brennan TA: **Can Practice Guidelines Reduce the Number and Costs of Malpractice Claims?**
JAMA 266:2856-2860, 1991

Gottlief SS, McCarter RJ, Vogel RA: **Effect of Beta-blockade on Mortality Among High-Risk and Low-Risk Patients After MI**.
NEJM, 339:489-497, 1998

Granville RL, Oshel RE: **The National Practitioner Data Bank Public Use File: A Valuable Resource for Quality Assurance Personnel and Risk Managers**.
Legal Med 98:4-9, 1998

Harris SJ: **Alternative Dispute Resolution: One Option to Avoid Court**.
Amer Med News 42:19, 1999

The Health Care Quality Improvement Act of 1986
42 U.S.C., Statute 11101-11152

Hirshfeld EB: **Should Practice Parameters be the Standard Of Care in Malpractice Litigation?**
JAMA 266:2886-2891, 1991

Jacobsen PD: **Legal and Policy Considerations In Using Clinical Practice Guidelines**.
Am J Cardiol 80: 74H-79H, 1997

Krumholz HM, Radford MJ, Wang Y, et. al: **National Use and Effectiveness of Beta-blockers for the Treatment of Elderly Patients After an MI**.
JAMA 280:623-629, 1998

McCullough, Campbell and Lande: **Summary of Medical Malpractice Law**.
www.mcandl.com 1998, accessed 12/9/99

Scott RW: *Health Care Malpractice – **A Primer on Legal Issues for Professionals***.
McGraw-Hill, N.Y., 1999

Simon RI: *Litigation Hot Spots in Clinical Practice.*
The Mental Health Practitioner and the Law.
Harvard University Press, Cambridge, 1998

Steinmetz DB, Steinmetz SP: **Proposed Changes in Malpractice Law – Are They Enough?**
Postgrad Med 95:93-97, 1994

Woolf SH: **Practice Guidelines: What the Family Physician Should Know**.
Amer Fam Physician 51:1455-1462, 1995

3. Risk Management

The information presented here is designed to supplement the **risk management (RM)** program that is already in place in your organization. The RM program will probably include the filing of occurrence screens, identification of sentinel events (anything causing death or serious injury), and a process termed root cause analysis. RM is also discussed in Chapter 10.

While RM is indirectly addressed in most of the articles and books on medicolegal issues, an understanding of the principles of risk management is important. Understanding the big picture provides the insight necessary to establish and maintain a healthy practice, from both a quality and a liability standpoint.

A good RM program is not limited to patient care issues, but addresses the effective functioning of the entire organization. It can also be successfully integrated into the organization's performance improvement program. Medical practice has many parallels with other risk-intensive organizations, such as industry. One reason for this is that medicine, by its very nature, is filled with uncertainty. Another reason is that physicians treat people who already have something wrong with them, and are at a higher risk than the rest of the population for becoming seriously ill or dying. There are many times when none of the choices doctors have to offer patients are particularly positive.

Definitions

Risk is the likelihood of incurring a loss or injury. RM is the process of minimizing risk. If a good RM program is in place, it offers both decision-making and data collection tools to ensure minimal standards of practice are met, and trends and opportunities for improvement identified.

Your very interest in this topic indicates a desire to reduce your risks. By understanding the liabilities unique to your current practice of medicine, you are less likely to overlook crucial factors.

Effective Risk Management Programs = Liability Reduction

All too often, medical organizations focus on risk management from a reactive and/or negative (that is, punitive) viewpoint. This is a bias born of the history of many RM programs. Previously, a variety of **Quality Assurance (QA)** programs were literally crammed down physician's throats. These programs began to spring up in the 1970's (immediately following the increase in medical malpractice suits). The majority of early QA programs were instituted with the aplomb of the "zero defect" mentality of those used in industry (prior to the Deming era). The person with the clipboard looking over everyone's shoulders was not a physician. It was widely thought that the goal of this individual was to find defects and errors, rather than asking for input to improve the process of providing quality care.

Although medical RM programs often only involve the process of identifying actual/potential problems in clinical practice after an untoward event has occurred, many industrial and military applications involve proactive programs. The practice of **risk analysis** (explained below) can be applied to the continuum of clinical practice – from administrative tasks to treatment. It offers an excellent mechanism for collecting data, assessing actual or potential problems, making changes, monitoring the effectiveness of various processes, and employing techniques found to be effective in one area of an organization in other areas. The process is as follows:

- Identify the (potential) problem, pending decisions, etc.

- Perform a **risk analysis**; this is the process of assessing a potential risk or negative event (after the fact) to establish its importance, to determine which resources should be devoted, and in what priority.

Risk Analysis (RA)

RA assesses the potential consequences of situations or events. **Severity** refers to the potential degree of injury, illness, property damage, or loss of resources that can result from a specified event. The combination of two or more events can dramatically increase the overall level of risk and severity of the outcome. To illustrate an RA exercise, a table can be drawn up containing categories of *outcome severity* and *likelihood of the event*:

Outcome Severity
Category I – The outcome may be a severe loss or death

Category II – The outcome may be severe injury, illness, or damage (personally or professionally)

Category III – The outcome may be minor injury, illness, or other damage

Category IV – The outcome presents a negligible possible loss

Outcome Likelihood

A – Likely to occur immediately or within a short period of time

B – Probably will occur in time (these are usually things that you can expect to occur)

C – May occur in time

D – Unlikely to occur

Once the severity and probabilities are assigned, insert these into a simple matrix and assign a risk code. For example:

	A	B	C	D
I	1	1	2	3
II	1	2	3	4
III	2	3	4	5
IV	3	4	5	5

Prioritizing With a Risk Code

Once you have established a risk code, it helps to prioritize your attention when you are faced with several choices. You can prioritize based on the RA numbers:

- 1 – "Do it now" (STAT/within 4 hours)
- 2 – "Do it soon" (48 – 72 hours)
- 3 – "Get to it when you can" (1 – 2 weeks)
- 4 – "Do it sometime" (6 months)
- 5 – "Do it after everything else is done, when you get the chance"

This simple system also allows you to compare two options from an RM standpoint, and logically select your priority. Many physicians perform this exercise intuitively – this exercise allows you to consciously go through the process and document your rationale.

The need to institute a clinical RM program is highlighted in the following scenario:

Your patient comes in for an annual physical exam, which includes a Pap test. When you review the chart, you realize that last year's cytology report isn't there. When you track it down, you discover that there were some dysplastic changes that should have been addressed by performing a repeat Pap test or a colposcopy (exact test based on the patient's specific circumstances).

You perform the appropriate work-up, and with a sigh of relief, note that the results are normal. If, on the other hand, the patient had suffered a progression of her disease, with some subsequent injury (e.g. a woman of childbearing age who now needs invasive surgical treatment that could have been avoided), you are now liable. Since it is your responsibility to ensure proper follow up of all ordered tests, you would, in all probability, lose the case.

A quick risk analysis for this situation is as follows:

1. Identify the problem – in this case, it is non-notification of lab/path results.

2. What is the likelihood this may happen again? Well, in all likelihood, it will occur again, chose 'B' from the above table.

3. How bad might the outcome be if it happens again? This is easy – it could be the direct cause of death to the patient and an indefensible major lawsuit to you. Chose 'I' from the table.

4. Plug these factors into your risk analysis chart and you have a '1,' a situation which needs to be addressed pronto.

Sometimes we all get caught up in the "squeaky wheel" issues, that if analyzed from a risk management perspective, are truly secondary to the welfare of your patients and your practice. This RA process can help you prioritize. As Stephen Covey recommends, spend more time in quadrants I and II, and less in quadrants III and IV.

Some Trouble Spots

A recent survey of physicians found that:

- 17 – 32% had no reliable method to make sure results of the tests they ordered were received

- 1/3 of the physicians did not always notify patients of abnormal lab results

- Only 23% of physicians reported having a reliable method for identifying patients who were overdue for follow-up

Assessing Your Practice

Look at your own practice environment and identify the areas or processes for which you need to institute appropriate safeguards.

Every clinical treatment entity, from a large **health maintenance**

organization (HMO) to a solo practitioner, should have a mechanism in place to identify *potential* and *actual* adverse events and to correct them. Any organization certified by the JCAHO must have an RM program. As a clinician, you are responsible for knowing what your organization's program is, and what your responsibilities are within the program. At the very least, you need to know when you must submit a report.

Most organizations have full-time or part-time risk managers. Take a moment to speak with them and find out about the program. Many physicians think of RM only as the proverbial "occurrence screen" you must complete when something goes wrong. If the RM program is effective, it will consist of a great deal more than this, and have some excellent resources for data collection, monitoring trends, and performance improvement ideas based on actual data (a novel concept!).

Potential issues in your practice can be identified through brainstorming sessions with what performance improvement folks call your "internal and external customers." These include the medical staff, nurses, office staff, administrators, consultants, suppliers, etc., (and perhaps a patient or two if appropriate). If you try to do this alone, you will only see one side of the strengths and weaknesses of your practice – a diverse group will identify many more. Two hours spent doing this will yield a multitude of benefits. If you have access to a trained risk manager, she can help with this exercise. If you do not, consider hiring a consultant. Many insurers offer inexpensive consulting for RM issues (remember, it's in their best interest to minimize your liability). Questions which may help generate some food for thought when doing your assessment are as follows:

- What are the top 5 – 10 diagnoses of this practice?
- What are the high-risk diagnoses?
- Which invasive procedures do we perform?
- What are the guidelines we should be following?
- What are our main confidentiality concerns?

- What are the possible conflict of interest issues in our practice?
- Do we have an effective feedback process for lab results, no shows, etc.?
- Do we have a **standard operating procedures (SOP)** manual that is updated annually?
- Do all staff receive mandatory training in all policies and procedures?
- Does our insurance provide full coverage for *all* our potential liabilities?
- Do we have a good understanding of the state and federal laws and regulations that affect our practice?
- Are our patient rights and responsibilities visibly posted?
- Is our charting and documentation adequate?
- Do we have a process to make use of patient complaints, potential problem identification, etc., for performance improvement?
- What are the five most common patient complaints?

When you've developed some facility with the above process, it becomes second nature, and requires only minimal additional administrative time. RM is addressed peripherally in many of the chapters of this book and almost every topic in this book is related to reducing risk.

Defensive Medicine

Defensive medicine is taking an action for the sole reason of limiting your liability in the case of a subsequent lawsuit. These are choices that you would not make if it weren't for the perception that you need to CYA (cover your anatomy). Most physicians report that they practice some form of defensive medicine. Examples are:

- Requesting a CT scan on every patient with a headache to make sure you don't miss a glioma

- Admitting patients to the hospital when they have *some* risk factors for suicide, although they aren't actively suicidal

- Ordering a complete blood count (CBC) on every patient because you once missed a case of leukemia

- Treating a child with a viral URI with antibiotics because the parents demand it

- Admitting all patients with chest pain to the cardiac care unit (CCU)

Some of these practices are not harmful to patients, they're just expensive. Other defensive practices can actually cause harm. Estimates are that the costs of defensive medicine are up to $10.6 billion dollars per year (even in the managed care environment of cost containment!).

If you have even a rudimentary RM program, you can make data-based decisions and still minimize risks without having to play the game of defensive medicine. A progress note containing your RA when comparing diagnostic or treatment options can go a long way toward supporting your decision in court (if it is ever challenged). Judges and juries are not fond of physicians who make treatment decisions based on reactive or subjective processes, rather than on data-based processes.

Three sources for further information about RM are the **American Society for Healthcare Risk Management (ASHRM)**, the JCAHO, and the NCQA.

Caveat
One of the absolute best risk management techniques you can establish is that of sharing uncertainty with your patients – remember, *share uncertainty and share risk.*

"When one finds oneself in a hole of one's own making, it is a good time to examine the quality of the workmanship."

John Renmerde

References

Benda CG, Rozovsky FA: *Liability and Risk Management in Managed Care,*
Aspen Press, Gaithersburg, Maryland, 1998

Bookaker EA, Ward RE, Uman JE, McCarthy BD: **Patient Notification and Follow-up of Abnormal Test Results: A Physician Survey.**
Arch of Intern Med 156:327-331, 1996

Carroll R: *Risk Management Handbook for Health Care Organizations, Second Edition.*
APHI, Chicago, 1997.

Crane M: **Once Burned, Twice Defensive.**
Medical Economics, 26 July 99

Fiscina S, Seifert JB: *Legal Check-up for Medical Practice – Essential Guide for the Healthcare Team.*
Mosby-Year Book, Inc., St. Louis, 1997

Gutheil TG, Bursztajn HJ, Brodsky A: **Malpractice Prevention Through the Sharing of Uncertainty: Informed Consent and the Therapeutic Alliance.**
NEJM 311:49-51, 1984

Reynolds RA, Rizzo JA, Gonzales ML: **The Costs of Medical Professional Liability**.
JAMA 257:2776, 1987

Author's Note: There is no single reference for the RA Process. Similar approaches are used in all branches of the military and in industry, and are considered common knowledge for those in high-risk environs. See the Resources Section for websites which contain RA information.

4. Doctor-Patient Relationships & Clinical Issues

The **doctor-patient relationship (DPR)** and related issues overlap both medicolegal and ethical realms, and are of prime importance to practicing clinicians. The topics in this chapter affect the multitude of interactions you have with your patients.

The scope of this chapter should not be considered to be all-inclusive, but presents the major areas in which clinicians need to have a good working knowledge. These areas include:

- **Informed Consent** (including determinations of the capacity to give informed consent)

- **The Right to Refuse Treatment**

- **Confidentiality** and **Privilege** (this section also addresses typical exceptions for confidentiality and the duty one has to third parties)

- **End of Life Issues** (this section focuses on the most crucial issues, as well as those that are often misunderstood and ethically difficult)

- **Boundary Issues** (particularly sexual relationships with patients, and dual relationships)

- **Abandonment**

- **False Imprisonment**

- **Good Samaritan Laws**

Informed Consent

Probably the most important communication issue that occurs between physicians and patients involves **informed consent (IC)**. While IC is well established as both an ethical and legal right of patients, its importance to successful DPRs cannot be overemphasized. Autonomy and the right of self-determination of each person are the fundamental ethical principles that apply to medical practice. These principles are at the very heart of medical ethics, and can assist decision-making in difficult areas of practice. Justice Cardoza eloquently presented this concept in a 1914 case, *"Every adult person of sound mind has the right to establish what is done with his own body."*

The practice of sharing uncertainty with patients is crucial in medical decision-making. IC means a two-way communication, and is never merely a signature on a piece of paper. Clinicians who are comfortable with the IC process respect the autonomy of their patients. Respecting autonomy means that practitioners must *know and understand* what their patients want, not *assume* to know what they would want in any particular situation.

IC is a legal and ethical doctrine that requires healthcare professionals to inform patients about their diagnoses, and the risks and benefits of various treatment options. Once it is clear that patients understand these aspects, they are allowed to make their choices, and clinicians must respect these decisions.

The Process of Obtaining IC

1. The patient is deemed to be capable of making medical decisions for himself (unless determined to be otherwise)

2. The patient is free of overt and covert coercion

3. The patient is fully informed about the following areas:

• the diagnosis and its implications

• the risks and benefits of the course of treatment being recommended

• the risks and benefits of alternative treatments

• the risks and benefits of receiving no treatment

The principle of **shared uncertainty** cannot be overemphasized. Almost everything that happens in medicine involves at least some degree of uncertainty. If patients understand the relative degree of uncertainty they face, they are much more likely to also accept the setbacks that may occur. Sharing uncertainty also distributes the responsibility between the patient and the physician on a more equal basis. In paternalistic times of yore, the doctor made the decisions and bore full responsibility for the consequences. This style of medical practice is neither appropriate nor wise.

Development of Informed Consent

Until the 1960's most of the medical malpractice cases fell under the "Oh My Gosh!" category (e.g. amputating the wrong leg), known as *res ipsa loquitor* (discussed in Chapter 2). IC cases were the first medical negligence lawsuits not actually based on the *res ipsa loquitor* kind of negligence. The standards currently in practice for IC cases developed primarily through several major precedent-setting cases. The presentation of three cases will illustrate how the current concept of IC developed, and highlight some of the ongoing problems facing clinicians.

Readers are reminded to check their state statutes regarding their exact requirements for obtaining IC. States vary significantly in their legal requirements, and most are lower than the recommended ethical standards. When addressing IC issues with patients, a guiding principle is to consider what you would want the doctor to tell you, your spouse, parent, sibling, etc. about any particular diagnosis or choice of treatment.

The first major precedent-setting case was that of *Natanson v. Kline*, a 1960 action involving radiation therapy that went awry. Mrs. Natanson had a radical mastectomy in 1955 for breast cancer. She then received cobalt radiation therapy to the mastectomy site and surrounding areas. Subsequently, her skin, flesh, and the muscles beneath her arm sloughed. Some of her ribs became necrotic. She and her husband testified that while they were told that the cobalt treatment was new, they were not informed of any potential danger. Mrs. Natanson was also given an excessive amount of radiation. Amazingly, the jury found for the defendants (physicians) in this case. On appeal, the jury was given the instruction by the judge (not given in the initial trial) that: *"the doctor must advise the patient of the nature of the proposed treatment and any hazards of the proposed treatment which are known to the physician."*

This was the first specific court requirement for IC, and established what is known as the **reasonable medical practitioner standard**. This means that *physicians have a duty to explain to patients what a reasonable, similarly trained physician would tell them under similar circumstances.*

Another important result of this case was stated as follows (and echoes Justice Cardoza's comments): *"Each man is considered to be master of his own body and he may, if he be of sound mind, expressly prohibit the performance of even life-saving surgery. A doctor might well believe that an operation is necessary, but the law does not permit him to substitute his own judgment for that of the patient by any form of deception."*

This comment foreshadowed future legal rulings, and is pertinent to the discussion of a patient's right to refuse treatment.

The **reasonable medical practitioner standard** was the accepted standard for informed consent until 1972, when the *Canterbury v. Spence* case established the **materiality of the information standard**. In this case, a 20-year-old male underwent a laminectomy for chronic pain. He was left a paraplegic. Afterwards, he said he was never told of the 1% risk of paraplegia accompanying the procedure. He also said that if he had been told, he would not have agreed to it. The *materiality of the information standard* means that *a patient must be told what any reasonable person would want to know to make a decision about the treatment or procedure.*

To have a successful case of medical negligence based on a violation of IC, it must be shown that the patient was not provided with the information mandated as necessary for that jurisdiction (a deviation from the SOC), and that the inadequate or lacking IC was the direct cause of the damage. The *Canterbury v. Spence* case clearly illustrates this connection – the patient claimed that if he had been told of the 1% risk of paraplegia, he would not have had the procedure, and would therefore not have become paraplegic. While there are frequent oversights in the IC process, it must be shown that: an injury occurred, and the lack of informed consent was clearly connected to that injury in order for the legal action to have merit.

Truman v. Thomas (1980) established the last aspect of the current requirements for IC. Dr. Thomas, a family practitioner, offered a Pap smear each year to Mrs. Truman. She declined the procedure because of the cost involved. She eventually developed an invasive cervical carcinoma and died. Her family sued Dr. Thomas, stating that he should have told her the risks of not having a Pap smear performed. He defended his actions by citing that the reason for having a Pap smear was common knowledge. The jury didn't agree. This case added to the IC requirements in that the risks and benefits (and prognosis) of *not* receiving treatment must be discussed, in addition to the risks and benefits of receiving a proposed course of treatment.

Caveat

The responsibility for obtaining IC from the patient cannot be delegated (even to another physician).

Ghost Surgery

Ghost surgery is a term describing an operation which is performed by a physician who is not named on the IC form. Remember, the assessment or treatment of patients without IC constitutes malpractice, and can actually make clinicians liable for the charge of battery – except where the law presumes consent (e.g. in an emergency). If the "right" surgeon operates on the wrong body part, or the "wrong" surgeon operates on the right body part, negligence can still be assessed in the event of an unfavorable outcome (though the other elements of negligence still need to be proven).

Ghost surgery lawsuits can also be filed under breach of contract and won easily in court if a surgeon promised to perform the operation personally (and didn't), or if the IC form doesn't include the surgeon who actually performed the procedure.

Remember, the requirements for the type, scope, and documentation of IC vary widely between jurisdictions. The majority of states use the objective, or the **reasonable person standard**. These statutes are worded such that as long as a "reasonable person" would have consented to the procedure or treatment, then a legal action based on improperly obtained IC cannot proceed. This type of statute prevents many frivolous lawsuits based on IC issues, but does not ensure that physicians meet their ethical obligations.

Some jurisdictions have a subjective standard which addresses individual patients (i.e. would this one person have proceeded with the treatment if full IC had been given?). This standard takes into account how different situations can affect people. Medical organizations should have specific policy guidelines on the scope of the IC process, which take into account the minimal legal standards for your jurisdiction. Each state outlines the treatments that absolutely require a signed document. The majority of states require a signed IC form for all invasive surgical procedures. Signed forms are very helpful in defense arguments (even when doctors don't fully explain the diagnosis, procedure, risks, benefits, alternatives, etc.).

Be cognizant of your jurisdictional requirements, but do not overlook ethical obligations. Remember that IC refers to the communication process you have with patients. It is best documented with good progress notes – not just a signature on a form.

Exceptions to Informed Consent

- Emergencies
- Therapeutic privilege
- Therapeutic waiver
- Implied consent

In emergency situations, the immediate care of the patient takes precedence over attending to procedural minutiae. If at all possible try to obtain consent from the patient's family.

An analogy to the axiom known as **Pascal's Wager** applies in emergency cases. Pascal's Wager (which is generally posed to those who are uncertain if God exists) refers to the premise that it is less risky to believe in God than to not. Once dead, if there is a God, the believer stands in good stead. If there is no God, nothing has been lost. If atheists discover after death that there indeed is a God they're not nearly as well positioned for a pleasant afterlife.

Similarly, when there is an emergency, acting quickly will always serve you in good stead, whereas not taking action (out of misguided fears of litigation) will not position you well. Acts of *omission* are just as potentially risky as acts of *commission*. Further, there is something particularly nasty about trying to defend a medical negligence case where the doctor failed to act because of what seemed like an administrative issue.

Caveat
Remember that all patients deemed to be mentally competent persons can refuse even life-saving treatment.

Therapeutic privilege describes the situation where physicians believe that telling patients about their condition, or the options of treatment, will worsen the situation. This should be used very rarely (if ever), and limited to cases where it seems highly likely that providing information will be harmful to patients.

An example of therapeutic privilege involves a patient who is admitted to the ICU after a massive MI complicated by recurrent ventricular tachycardia. One might not want to mention that the MI has progressed until after the arrhythmia is controlled.

An illegal and unethical use of therapeutic privilege would involve not telling a schizophrenic patient about the risk of tardive dyskinesia (which can occur following treatment with the traditional antipsychotics). A well-intentioned psychiatrist cannot use the exception of therapeutic privilege by saying, "if the patient knew about the risk, she wouldn't take the medication." It may well be that the patient wouldn't accept treatment even with the clear benefits that could be realized. Situations such as these are not considered a valid enough reason to take away a person's right to self-determination. If a schizophrenic patient lacks the capacity to make medical decisions, then her guardian/

surrogate will make the decision (again, in accordance with the state laws that apply in this situation).

You do not need to tell the patient about every possible side effect of a treatment or procedure, only the most common and the most serious ones. Remember to focus on the risks and benefits that a reasonable person would want to know to be able to make the decision.

Therapeutic waiver is the other exception to the legal requirement for informed consent. This occurs when a patient says that he doesn't want to be told anything about his condition or recommended treatment. If a patient says something like: "Oh doctor, I don't understand all of your medical talk and don't want to know. You're so smart – you make all the decisions for me" – look out! This situation is a potential landmine. If a patient says this, tell him that you believe it is much better for him to at least try to understand the treatment options, and to consider inviting a family member to join the discussion.

If the patient absolutely refuses to be involved in the process, and is competent to make that decision, get a witness (someone other than a family member) to corroborate your discussion. Make sure you document the conversation (and the name of the witness) in the medical record.

Caveat
The type of patient who wants others to make decisions for her frequently possesses dependent personality traits, and may well harbor passive resentments as well. In the event of an unfavorable outcome, the patient (and family) may become very angry. What you want to avoid is having this resentment directed at you, and eventually unburdened in the courtroom (i.e. "The doctor never told me"). Don't let yourself get "set-up."

The IC process is the cornerstone of good patient care, and this involves respecting autonomy. If the patient is part of the ongoing decision-making process, he very likely has a strong alliance with the treatment team, feels listened to, and is much less likely to pursue litigation as a course of action (even in the event of an unfavorable outcome). When patients believe that they have been ignored, misled, given only cursory attention, or not treated with respect, angry (and litigious) feelings are likely to arise.

Implied consent. When a patient holds out her arm to get blood drawn, this implies consent for the venipuncture. Implied consent as an exception to IC covers undisclosed risks that are considered common knowledge (once again, by the omnipresent, "reasonable" person).

Documenting Informed Consent

Documentation plays an important role in IC and its many offshoots (such as the right to refuse treatment). More information on documentation is presented in Chapter 5.

Clinicians know that good documentation is imperative – not only as an RM issue, but to ensure good patient care. Other providers need to know information about medications, allergies, diagnoses, etc. Unfortunately, many physicians have been exposed to the "castor oil" theory of documentation (i.e. if the documentation wasn't perfect, the entire scope of care was criticized). This approach is discouraging for training physicians (and may cause a "purging" of the desire to improve). When something unpleasant is forced on anyone, it is human nature to reject it, even if it might ultimately be something positive. The bottom line is:

- Good notes do help the patient
- If you didn't document it – "it" never happened
- Write smarter, not more
- If it can't be read, it won't help you or anyone else

As students, many physicians were told they needed better documentation skills. The natural reaction is to write longer notes. The phrase "just the facts, ma'am!" is particularly valid in this situation. You do not have to write a short story about the 15 minute talk you had with a patient – just the basics of their symptoms, your assessment, and management plan. If there was anything added to the treatment plan, a brief documentation of the IC process is in order. Most items need only a few sentences.

It is particularly valuable to make a record of the questions that patients have. This provides clear documentation of the patient's participation in the IC process, and that you addressed their questions. The following is an example of a progress note on a patient who suffers from depression, and records the process of initiating an antidepressant medication:

ID: 32-year-old MCF followed for treatment of major depression. Takes only oral contraceptive pills. Denies allergies to medications.

Subjective: Seen 2 weeks ago for symptoms of depression in the context of marital discord. Returns today after starting marital counseling. Currently suffering from insomnia (early a.m. awakening), fatigue, tearfulness, feelings of worthlessness, and diminished concentration. Denied suicidal ideation. No new stressors.

Objective: Neatly groomed, cooperative, appears tired; soft-spoken with psychomotor retardation (slumped in chair/slowed gait); "pretty down" mood with blunted, dysphoric affect – appropriate to expressed thought process. Denies suicidal ideation. No evidence of psychosis. Beck Depression Inventory – 28; TSH 1.2.

Assessment: Major Depressive Disorder, single episode, moderate severity, without psychotic features (DSM-IV 296.22)

Management Plan:
1. Begin fluoxetine 20 mg, p.o., qam. Discussed most common side effects – sleepiness/anxiety, nausea/anorexia, headache. Explained other first-line meds and probable course with and without meds. Told she needed to stay on meds for 6 to 9 months after resolution of symptoms.

2. Patient to call in one week; follow-up in 2 weeks. To continue marital/individual counseling with social worker.

3. Patient to call in the interim with any questions/concerns.

4. Agreed to contact me or the ER if she develops suicidal ideation in the interim. She is competent to make treatment decisions.

5. Patient Education: Watched videotape on depression – expressed surprise at how classic her symptoms were and said she felt more hopeful after seeing the tape.

6. Patient expressed an understanding of the above treatment plan and process of recovery.

Competence/Capacity to Make Medical Decisions

While the exact wording of IC statutes vary between jurisdictions, there is one absolute. For IC to be considered valid, the person giving it must be competent to do so. All adults are presumed to be competent unless there is a legitimate reason to think otherwise. The underlying assumption is that the person considering treatment is able to do so under the umbrella of protection provided by the ethical and legal doctrine of **self-determination**. Because of this, many physicians don't mention that the patient was deemed competent when IC was obtained. Making a notation in the medical record that a patient was deemed capable of providing IC can be very beneficial. Cases where competency is a potential issue usually involve the following situations:

- A patient agrees to a treatment that has a low potential benefit and a moderate potential risk

- A patient refuses a treatment that has a low risk and a significant potential benefit

- The patient's family disagrees with the treatment plan

- The patient agrees to a research protocol

- The patient's record has evidence that could raise the question of competency (e.g. a nurse's note recording decreased cognitive awareness at night, after meds, etc.)

- IC was given after the patient took medication that could affect memory, judgment, cognition, etc. (to avoid this situation, it is best to have the IC discussion before the patient receives medication)

- Any other situation where you want to make sure the patient is competent to provide informed consent

Some background information about competency determinations is as follows:

Competence refers to having the capacity to understand and act reasonably. Competence is a legal term, and the decision about someone's competence is made by a judge.

Capacity is having the mental ability to make a rational decision (based on understanding and appreciating all relevant information). Capacity is determined by a clinician.

There are many different types of competency (over 30) that can be adjudged. In general, when there is more at stake for an individual (e.g. loss of life or liberty, finances, etc.), a higher level of evidence indicating competence is required.

Areas of Competence
This list is compiled in approximate decreasing order of stringency:

- Execution

- Stand Trial – the accused must understand what he is being charged with, the role of the major figures in the courtroom (i.e. what the jury does, etc.), and be able to participate in his or her own defense

- Be Sentenced

- Manage Financial Affairs – a person must know the basics of what something costs, how items are paid for, the general nature of their assets, etc., although it is not required that the person makes sound financial decisions

- Live Independently – the person must be able to list the important aspects of how to live safely on his or her own (i.e. how to find a place to stay, how to find food, remember to turn off the stove, etc.)

• Make Medical Decisions

• Enter Into a Contract – this requires an understanding of what a contract involves, and what is at risk

• Be A Witness (**Testimonial Capacity**) – this often becomes an issue when a child is required to give testimony

• Get Married – this requires an understanding of what marriage means, and the general responsibilities required of a spouse

• Vote – political commentary aside. . . albeit tempting

• Make A Will *(***Testamentary Capacity***)* – this involves one of the lowest standards of evidence. People are generally allowed to do what they want to do with their money, regardless of how eccentric others may find the decision. In general, a person's wishes are carried out as long as there was no coercion or undue influence at the time the will was written. Testamentary capacity requires: that the person knows a will is being made; an approximate understanding of net worth; identity of the natural heirs; and in some jurisdictions, an understanding of the potential impact that financial decisions would have on "usual" heirs.

Each of these "competencies" are assessed by balancing an individual's constitutional rights against local laws and the interests of society.

In most jurisdictions, attending physicians are legally able to be the "capacity assessors" for their patients. However, the majority of physicians, unless trained in the assessment process, do not understand how to proceed, and are wise to request assistance from a consultant.

When a consultant (usually a psychiatrist or psychologist) is asked to "do a capacity assessment," it is important to clarify which type of capacity needs to be assessed, and for what specific reason. These are crucial elements, because "capacity" is specific to a person's decision-making ability for a *specific task* at a *specific time*. (e.g. to assess Mr. Langerhans capacity to consent to an ERCP scheduled for tomorrow). There are mental health professionals who do not know how to conduct capacity assessments. For this reason, it is prudent to ensure that your consult request is directed to someone who has the proper training and experience.

An error frequently made by clinicians is to equate a patient's decision-making capacity with her performance on the **mini-mental state exam (MMSE)**. While most researchers agree that scores of less than 20 (out of 30) on the MMSE provide a fairly good correlation with a lack of decision-making capacity, this alone is not sufficient evidence. Also, up to one-third of patients with impairments in their decision-making ability (overlooked by physicians) will score between 20 – 30 on the MMSE. Many people have impaired decision-making abilities that are disguised by cognitive abilities which remain intact.

The capacity to make medical decisions balances the competing interests of doing no harm to the patient against preserving the right to self-determination. The principle underlying the concept of IC is that each person, while deemed competent, has the right to make decisions regarding her medical care, even if others consider these decisions to be unwise. This principle is at times difficult for physicians to accept.

Many authors who write in the area of medical decision-making capacity believe in the usefulness of a "sliding scale," where different types of capacity require varying levels of decision-making ability. In other words, the more there is at risk for the patient, the more physicians will want to be certain that the patient has intact decision-making capacity. While a sliding scale is not an officially recognized legal consideration, it does have widespread acceptance.

Example of a Sliding Scale for Decision-Making Capacity

A patient is offered a medication that will likely cause few side effects, and is potentially of life-saving benefit. Here, a physician might be less concerned about the patient's capacity to accept treatment because there is little risk involved and considerable benefit. However, when a treatment is proposed that has high likelihood of causing side effects or complications, coupled with little potential benefit, it is critical to establish that the patient is competent to make medical decisions.

A major undertaking in the study of capacity determinations has involved the area of participation in clinical research. This is a particular concern when the research subjects have questionable capacity (e.g. involuntary patients or those with mental impairment) or where there is the potential for coercion (or the perception of coercion). Doctors who recruit their own patients for research that they themselves are conducting must be careful. Should patients have even the perception that they are being coerced, physicians may be on shaky ethical and legal grounds. Patients may harbor covert fears that by not participating, they may fall out of favor with their doctor, and compromise the quality of their care. Many physicians consider it a conflict of interest to recruit their own patients.

Capacity assessments have been performed for decades on two groups of patients: those participating in clinical research, and those who have been hospitalized on an involuntary basis (usually on psychiatric units). However, in other areas of medicine, this has been a relatively recent focus. For readers interested in this area, the reference section lists articles by Drs. Appelbaum and Grisso, which are of particular assistance. While several approaches for conducting capacity assessments exist, the schema provided by Drs. Appelbaum and Grisso has been widely used and validated, and is easily integrated with the legal standards for competency.

Since competence is a legal term, most jurisdictions require that patients demonstrate the following capabilities in order to be considered competent to make medical decisions:

- The ability to express a choice (Section A)

- The ability to understand the information (B)

- The individual's ability to appreciate the information as it applies to her specific case (C) – this is not required in all jurisdictions

- The ability to reason with the information (D)

A. The ability to express a choice involves: the patient *being capable* of making a decision about his care, *arriving* at such a decision, and *informing* someone of that decision. This is not always as simple as saying 'yes' or 'no.'

Patients do not necessarily have to communicate their decisions verbally. Patients on ventilators may be able to communicate via blinking, writing, hand squeezing, etc. Non-verbal patients are frequently "written off" as being unable to participate in healthcare decisions.

A somewhat more subtle problem can arise with submissive, dependent individuals who are unable or unwilling to make decisions. In situations involving ambivalent patients, the underlying cause of their uncertainty needs to be explored – is it because the individual received new information and made a valid reassessment of the situation, or is it because auditory hallucinations are confusing them? Again, the sliding scale of competency is an important consideration.

If someone is completely unable to express a choice because of a mental or physical illness, then a guardian needs to be appointed to make medical decisions. If a patient is merely ambivalent, or has trouble making decisions, the resolution depends on the degree of risk involved in the decision. A referral to a psychiatric colleague can be particularly useful in cases where the etiology of someone's ambivalence is unclear.

B. A patient's ability to understand information is the aspect of capacity that receives the most attention from physicians. If it is obvious that the patient doesn't understand what the physician is saying, the issue of IC is called immediately into question. At some point during the interview, a physician will ask, "Mr. Jones, do you understand the things I've just told you?" If the patient says "no," or has a blank stare, few doctors would be comfortable with a signed consent form.

C. The next item is often less well understood or considered in the process of capacity determination. In addition to understanding the information provided by physicians, a patient must be able to **appreciate how this information pertains to his case**. While a patient may seem to be cognitively intact and have a good understanding of facts presented, he may not appreciate how the facts pertain to him specifically. An example is as follows:

Mrs. Brown is in the ER for evaluation of a possible placenta praevia. She seems to understand the need for an emergency cesarean section. The difficulty arises when her doctor leans forward to get her signature after detailing the risks to her, and she states, "Wait a minute! I understood what you were saying doc, but it doesn't apply to me – I'm not pregnant!

Frequently, people with delusional disorders, selective neurologic deficits, etc. appear entirely normal. Their lack of decision-making capacity goes unrecognized unless a thorough assessment is undertaken.

D. The final aspect of assessing capacity is an evaluation of the patient's **ability to reason with the information provided**. This is particularly important when a patient makes a choice that is not seen as "reasonable," or not one that most people would make. As long as a patient can coherently explain why a certain choice is being made, provide a clear understanding of the possible implications, and demonstrate how the situation applies to her personally, then physicians must respect the choice being made.

Competence to make medical decisions is an increasingly important concept for physicians to understand, practice, and document.

It is crucial for anyone performing a capacity assessment to ensure that the patient has been fully informed about her condition and proposed treatment beforehand. Sitting in with the treating physician and listening to the information provided is one way of accomplishing this. If you are the treating physician who has requested the consult, it can be very helpful to go through the elements of IC with the patient one more time. It is perfectly appropriate to re-educate someone again at the time of a capacity assessment. The goal of the IC is to support the autonomy of patients, and as far as possible, allow them to make their own choices. You don't want to remove their right to make decisions unless there is clear evidence of incapacity.

Special Issues
Research
Much has been written in the area of the ethical, legal, and moral rights and wrongs of performing research on those who

may be only marginally competent (or even incompetent). Even for clearly competent patients, many checks and balances are available.

There is a specified department under the **Department of Health and Human Services (DHHS)**, which oversees research conducted that uses federal funding; this is the **Office for Protection for Research Risks (OPRR)**. Many federally funded organizations have received suspensions for a variety of violations, such as the use of ineligible patients, using coercion, or using inadequate means to obtain IC.

Most organizations are required (by policy or law) to have strict processes in place to oversee human research. This may include a Committee for the Protection of Human Subjects, an **Institutional Review Board (IRB)**, etc. All human research funded by the DHHS and the FDA must be approved by an IRB.

The University of Rochester has a unique training program. The principal researchers must take an exam (and score at least 85%) to have their studies made eligible for IRB review. The OPRR is available to answer questions about specific situations, from either IRB members or individuals.

Recent protocols on **Alzheimer's Disease (AD)** patients are illustrative examples of competing ethical issues and their appropriate resolution. On one hand, patient rights activists are vocal about protecting individuals who lack the ability to give IC. On the other hand, those in the early stages of AD (and a different set of activists) state that not performing research on this disabling illness is discriminatory.

Like all other issues where the rights of individuals are considered, the potential benefits must be weighed against foreseeable risks. The **National Institute of Mental Health (NIMH)** has developed a protocol that satisfies both groups.

Patients in the early stages of AD are assessed for their capacity to consent to participate in research studies. At that time, when still able to make decisions about their treatment and research involvement, they appoint a surrogate to make these decisions for them when they are no longer able to do so. There are many safeguards built into this process (such as not performing a procedure if there is evidence that the subject is in any kind of discomfort, etc.). The NIMH has developed a very satisfactory approach by using **advance directives**. This allows patients to maintain their autonomy and protect those who do not have adequate decision-making capacity.

Patients must be free of coercion in order to give consent to participate in research. Previously, a large amount of research was conducted on "captive" populations – prisons, mental institutions, and the military. The past few decades have seen huge legal changes designed to protect the rights of these populations. The Nuremberg Principles, developed after the atrocities performed in the name of research during the Holocaust, are used by many organizations to ensure adherence to the highest ethical standards.

Even if DHHS funding is not provided, it is appropriate to follow their basic guidelines (and use JCAHO standards for guidance, whether or not you are part of a JCAHO-accredited organization).

Concern about coercion also applies to individual physicians who conduct research, particularly regarding recruitment. How can physicians recruit subjects from their own patient pool without even the slightest degree of coercion? Even if a physician says, "I made sure she knew she didn't have to participate," many patients have a desire to please their physicians and are afraid that their care might suffer if they don't participate.

Research efforts have also focused on patients with psychiatric illnesses and their capacity to give consent to participate in research studies.

Minors

Physicians who care for minors and adolescents need to be aware of both state laws and local facility policies regarding the capacity to consent to research, obtaining IC, etc. In most jurisdictions, the parents are the child's guardians, and have decision-making responsibility. If the parents are divorced, the parent with primary custody has the responsibility for consenting to treatment. Be aware that you cannot release information to the non-custodial parent without proper consent.

While parents ultimately make decisions for minors, physicians should still make every effort to explain the diagnosis and treatment to the child. Even though the legal decision-making responsibility lies with the parent, there are ethical responsibilities to both the parent and the child.

Economic Informed Consent

This topic is discussed in more detail in Chapter 6, but it deserves mention here. The concept of economic informed consent is fairly new. Although not yet a legal requirement, many believe it is indeed an ethical mandate. Managed care, in theory, focuses on providing *adequate* care while containing costs.

Economic informed consent refers to the ethical requirement to disclose all appropriate treatments, not only those authorized by the patient's health plan. Physicians should also disclose any potential financial gain they will receive from recommending treatment options (this is an ethical, and in some cases legal requirement).

Caveats for Informed Consent

A valuable question to ask patients is what their expectations are for treatment. For example, ask the following questions, "What does success mean to you in this situation?" or "What do you hope to get from treatment?" This will help differentiate what you think success is from what the patient envisions.

An example is as follows. A 68-year-old cancer patient has a reasonable chance of survival (for several years) by accepting an aggressive chemo/radiation therapy regimen (that will make him feel lousy). When you ask this patient what he hopes to gain from the treatment, he may state, "I want to have a few good pain-free months to spend with my family and finish a few paintings." This informs you which aspects to emphasize in your discussion about treatment options. You can still offer your preferred treatment plan, but you now know where the priority of the patient lies – quality vs. quantity of time remaining.

Another suggestion is to ask patients to list their top three priorities or goals in seeking medical care. For one it may be minimizing pain, another to allow mobilization, and others would want to be able to live independently.

The Right to Refuse Treatment

The right to refuse treatment is intertwined with the IC process, but at times seems much less straightforward. Remember, the autonomy of the patient reigns supreme in making medical decisions (when the patient is deemed competent). It is every person's right to make unwise decisions and to refuse treatment that may even be lifesaving. In the latter instance, the patient is choosing one of the treatment alternatives (which is to receive no treatment). Right to refuse treatment issues are on a continuum with right to die issues (addressed later in this chapter).

Leaving Hospital Against Medical Advice (AMA)

Some patients want to leave hospital when it is against medical advice (AMA). An example of this situation is as follows:

It is Friday night at 8 p.m., and you are trying to finish your own rounds and leave. You are called to see a patient (not your own, of course) who is having a heated discussion with a nurse. The patient ripped out her IV, and also has her angry spouse with her. The nurse hands you an AMA release, and asks you to have Mrs. Jones sign it. This situation is a set-up for an unfavorable outcome, which may well be accompanied by lingering feelings of animosity. It doesn't have to be this way. One approach to this problem is as follows:

First, get a concise history about what is going on. Then, see the patient immediately, and say something like the following: "Hello Mrs. Jones, my name is Dr. Wear-Finkle (shake hands). I hear that you wish to leave the hospital. Is it OK if I talk with you for a few minutes?" (at this point sit down across from Mrs. Jones) "What is the reason that you are upset and want to leave hospital?"

Your job in this encounter is to attempt to understand why Mrs. Jones wants to leave. It often has nothing to do with quality of care issues, but rather a negative personal interaction with one of the staff, possibly coupled with the patient's fears. You can take the interaction from an adversarial one to at least neutral ground. If the problem cannot be fixed with an empathetic and non-challenging intervention, and you believe that Mrs. Jones is competent to make an informed decision to leave the hospital, she can of course leave. It is important that you ensure that she knows the following (which you document in the record):

- Her diagnosis

- The reasons you recommended further hospitalization

- The risks she faces by leaving the hospital without continued treatment

- That she was told she could return for further treatment at the facility

- The symptoms for which she should seek immediate care, and the risks of ignoring these symptoms

- Other possible places she can receive treatment if she chooses not to return to your hospital

Any resemblance to the previous doctrine of IC is entirely intentional! The AMA process is the same as IC, where a competent patient has the right to choose between the available treatment options – one of these options being to decline treatment altogether.

If your organization insists that the patient sign an "AMA Form" then ask her to do so. Simply state that the form is a record that the patient understands she is leaving against the advice of medical personnel. Much more important than this form is a well-written note in the medical record containing the points listed above. Note the patient's capacity to make this decision, particularly if she is refusing treatment that places her at high risk upon leaving the facility.

Physicians cannot prevent a competent patient from leaving the hospital, regardless of whether this decision appears to be an act of poor judgment. If the patient's competence is in question, perform a capacity assessment, and follow your organizational and jurisdictional guidelines.

False Imprisonment

False imprisonment occurs when a competent patient is prevented from leaving a health care facility, or is committed to an institution in violation of state law. Patients do not have to be locked in solitary confinement to be falsely imprisoned. If physical restraints are applied, or someone is forcibly prevented from leaving the ER and there is no legal indication for this, the person may sue everyone involved for both false imprisonment and battery. False imprisonment actions make for clear and simple, no-fuss lawsuits. This is an intentional tort, not a negligence action. There is no requirement to prove the *dereliction of duty/direct causation of damages* aspect – only that the person was restrained against his or her will without justification.

A tragic case that clearly illustrates this issue is that of a 29-year-old woman with a lifelong history of asthma. She presented to an ER for treatment. She authorized only treatment with oxygen, but was given both oxygen and another medication by nebulizer. She developed a headache from the medication, removed the mask, and expressed her desire to leave the ER. The staff was concerned about her oxygenation status, and the doctor felt she would need to be intubated. He told her he would treat her in a conservative fashion. The patient and her sister didn't trust the doctor and instead decided to leave. They were stopped at the exit by a security guard and a doctor, and forcibly separated. The patient was physically restrained and intubated. She did not give consent for the intubation. When she was released from the hospital the next day, she felt traumatized, and stated she would never again go to a hospital. Two years later, she again had a severe attack and refused to go for treatment. When she lost consciousness, an ambulance was summoned, but she died two days later.

Her father sued the physician and the hospital for the events that had transpired during the intial ER visit. His lawsuit alleged wrongful death, negligence, assault and battery, false imprisonment, and a violation of his late daughter's civil rights. The trial judge instructed the jury that a patient has the right to refuse medical treatment except in a life-threatening emergency situation. The jury found for the defendants.

On appeal to the Supreme Judicial Court of Massachusetts, the lower court ruling was reversed. To this court, it was clear that a competent patient has the right to refuse treatment, even when faced with a life-threatening situation.

Confidentiality

"Three may keep a secret when two of them are dead."

Benjamin Franklin

Confidentiality is the Clinician's Obligation to keep information obtained in a professional relationship from third parties, unless the patient authorizes its release. This is both an ethical and a legal requirement.

Breach of confidentiality suits are not unusual. Even if the physician was not directly involved, he or she may be considered responsible because of the principle of vicarious liability (remember the deep pocket theory of litigation). For example, if the event in question was due to a negligent office practice or an action by one of the staff, the physician can still be held liable. The deeper pockets of the health care organization, if it didn't ensure that its policies were clearly promulgated, could also be targeted in a lawsuit.

Some of the most common places where breaches of confidentiality occur are the hospital cafeteria, elevators, and doctors' offices. A rule of thumb is to assume that the person standing next to you in a public place knows the person whose case you intend to discuss, and will tell the patient exactly what you said.

Don't leave medical records in sight of anyone who may be in your office (and may get nosy if you leave). Politely ask someone to leave your office if you need to take a telephone call.

One surprising tidbit to consider if you are responsible for the confidentiality of an office practice is the following: if your administrative staff did everything correctly with regard to not leaving records out, but forgot to lock the area where the records are kept, you may still be liable. If someone enters a closed area and opens an unlocked file cabinet to view a record that is in your safekeeping, *you are liable*, not the trespasser. Even though the other person was trespassing, as long as he didn't have to "break and enter" to gain access to records, the responsibility is yours.

Information Management

This is a huge new area in both medicine and office management. Electronic records present valuable opportunities to improve care, but also many possibilities for breaches of confidentiality. If you are making the transition to an electronic record in your practice, ensure the software company has clear procedures to safeguard the security of the information.

Frequently Overlooked Areas
Office Procedures

The next time you enter your clinical areas, check the following items:

Telephone answering machines
What is your arrangement for voice mail? Is the answering machine in a secure area? If not, is the volume turned down? Who listens to the messages, and where does this occur? The important thing is to ensure that only those who have a need to know information about patients are in a position to hear it.

Computer security
Who has access to the computers? Are patient records (and sensitive information) protected by a password?

Computer servicing
What happens when the computer needs to leave the office to be serviced? Would anyone think to clear all personal records from the hard drive?

Are the medical records in a file cabinet that locks?
Although it is hard to imagine someone riffling through records, it does happen. Backup computer disks should also be kept in a locked area.

Day-to-day practice
When patients enter the office, are there patient records open

(or even on your desk if you leave the room)? Is any patient information on the computer screen?

Voice pagers
Make certain that the volume is turned down so the incoming message is not within earshot of others. If the lab announces your CEO's positive gonorrhea culture over your pager during an executive meeting, this can be a career-limiting event.

Disposal of confidential information
Ensure that the process you think is happening, is actually taking place. It is not unheard of that medical record contents are sorted into piles by prisoners and sold to the highest-bidding recycler.

Exceptions to the Confidentiality of Medical Records

The legal requirement for confidentiality does not apply in the following situations:

Duties to Third Parties

- When your patient is a threat to others

Mandatory Reporting

- Communicable diseases
- Child or elder abuse
- Impaired driving
- Any other mandatory reportable item in your
  jurisdiction

Mandatory reporting can be a very sticky area – know which statutes say "shall" or "may" or "shall not."

If you fail to report something when you are required to do so, you may face disciplinary action. Alternatively, if you make a report and are not required to (or are prohibited from doing so), you may face civil action. In Florida, for example, spouse abuse cannot be reported without the victim's permission. The requirement to report gunshot wounds or other wounds indicating violence is in force only when the physician was actually called to treat the wound, not finding them as an incidental discovery during another exam.

Court-Ordered Requests

This can occur as part of any criminal trial, a civil suit, or at the request of an administrative body (like a licensing board or as part of a workman's compensation hearing). The crucial issues in this instance are that you:

- Inform the patient about the limits of confidentiality in
  your evaluation

- Outline exactly who will have access to the written
  report

- Discuss the potential impact of the evaluation

Clearly, IC is required to be able to conduct the evaluation. Several physicians have been burned by doing an evaluation for a workman's compensation claim, releasing the information to the employer, and then being sued for breach of confidentiality.

Patient-Litigant

This means that the patient has raised the condition(s) for which you are treating them as part of litigation. Once the individual has placed his or her condition *at issue*, you are no longer bound to keep information confidential (in reality, it means that privilege can no longer be invoked – this is also described below). Despite this, seek legal counsel before releasing any confidential information.

Dual Agency

There are several settings where the physician has a duty to both the patient and an organization. This most frequently occurs in prisons, the military, and schools. The patient should be told ahead of time by the doctor that the usual level of confidentiality does not apply in this particular situation. Again, this is principally an issue of IC. Most physicians working in these environments are aware of their ethical duties to the patient populations they serve. It may come as a surprise to many who do not work in these systems, but there is a strong focus on the preservation of individual rights despite the competing interests.

Duties to Third Parties

This term refers both to the duty to protect others from the actions of your patients, and the legal duty you may unintentionally incur from your actions. It is important to have an awareness of both factors, and to be able to distinguish between the two. Psychiatrists and other mental health professionals are well aware of the duty they have to third parties when one of their patients indicates the desire to harm another person. This **duty to warn/duty to protect** a clearly identifiable third party from harm is addressed in all state legislation. This duty developed from the 1974 & 1976 Tarasoff cases:

Tatiana Tarasoff was a student at the University of California who casually befriended an Indian student named Prosenjit Poddar. Following the customary behavior of his culture, he believed they were betrothed when she kissed him. She subsequently rejected him, and he felt betrayed. He told a psychologist at the university counseling center that he had thoughts of killing her. The psychologist notified the campus police, who questioned and released Poddar when he denied that he intended any harm. At the time, Tatiana was out of the country for a semester. Poddar befriended Tatiana's brother. When she returned to the university, he stalked her and killed her. Her family sued everyone involved. The primary issue was whether she and her family should have been warned by the counseling center and the police about the possible risk of being harmed. The 1974 verdict established the **duty to warn** an identified victim. The 1976 finding established a **duty to protect** the intended victim (which allows for a variety of interventions, including hospitalization). A unique aspect to this tragic story was that the psychologist told the supervising psychiatrist about his concerns, and the psychiatrist's response was to destroy all pertinent records. Not wise.

Individual state requirements vary widely. Even in states where the statute is worded to say that an identified victim "may" be warned "if" the patient has the means and "is more likely than not to act on the intent" – common sense dictates that at some point there is an ethical duty to protect others. This surpasses the patient's right to confidentiality – statute or no statute. Know your state laws and then decide what you can live with.

Caveat
"I would much prefer to defend a breach of confidentiality suit than a wrongful death suit!"

A Famous Defense Lawyer

This is an ideal place to apply an RA to assist you in making a decision in the tough cases.

1. If you act to protect someone from your patient, you risk making the patient angry and being sued for a possible breach of confidentiality. However, the way you take such an action can minimize this risk. Try to find a way to inform your patient of your concern and intent to notify others in a way that doesn't destroy the treatment alliance.

2. If you do not take action, and your patient kills or severely injures another person, you risk a much "higher stakes" lawsuit, as well as other emotional and professional losses.

A risk analysis would look something like this (refer to the table on page 47):

1. The severity of the potential problem would be a 'III' (patient angry and possible breach of confidentiality suit). The likelihood of the patient being angry is high, so choose 'B' (can expect a problem). The risk code on the grid is a '3' – which is "a problem which can be dealt with in a reasonable time period."

2. The severity of the potential problem would be a 'I' (patient killing or injuring someone with big-time consequences). The likelihood would be either a 'B' (expected to happen), or a 'C' (may occur in time). Either way, the risk code will be '1' (uh-oh!) or '2' (better get on it), both of which are higher than the '3' in the first option.

It is particularly helpful to apply an RA to any issue that is emotionally charged, and for which there is no single, clear solution. Courts have usually used common sense (yes, it's true) in the above situations. They will usually side with the clinician who acted in good faith to try to protect others.

Caveat

All duties to third parties are based on protecting identifiable or, at times, even non-identifiable persons from the foreseeable harmful acts of your patients.

As noted in the exceptions to confidentiality section above, a duty can be established when you have knowledge that your patient may pose a foreseeable risk to others (either identifiable persons, or others in general). The extent and scope of your duty in different situations is dictated by state and case law. A good example is the risk of HIV⁺ patients transmitting the virus. Some states require reporting or that the sexual partner be notified. Some states allow physicians to make the notification, others states forbid notification altogether.

Release of Information to Third Parties

Whatever your practice milieu, it is prudent to know your facility guidelines regarding release of information to third parties. Always ask patients to sign a release of information form. As with all forms that may have eventual liability importance, legal counsel should check it for completeness and appropriateness.

Caveat
Except in rare situations, do not release any patient information without signed consent.

As discussed above, there are limited situations in which a physician can release information when not authorized to do so by the patient:

- *State Reporting Requirements.* All states have a variety of required reports. These include, but are not limited to: communicable diseases; child, spouse or elder abuse; gunshot wounds; etc.

- *HIV.* Know your local reporting requirements. Violating established HIV reporting procedures is a major potential liability issue.

- *Department of Motor Vehicles (DMV).* Many states have mandatory reporting for several conditions, while others require that the department be notified of those for whom there is a concern, and then they conduct an investigation into the person's ability to safely operate a vehicle.

Notifying the DMV is not always a clear-cut decision, and involves weighing the evidence for impairment against removing a personal freedom. The best way for any physician to deal with these issues is to discuss matters with the patient. In many instances, the patient will be reasonable and agree to give up driving or restrict her time on the road. The second avenue of pursuit is to include family members. If there is still concern, tell the patient that you are notifying the DMV. If you have dealt with this matter in a fair and progressive manner with the patient, you are unlikely to be faulted for erring on the side of safety.

Minors

Familiarize yourself with your state laws regarding the release of information involving minors. Be clear as to whether your patients may be an **emancipated minor** (which is adjudged by a court). Emancipated minors have all the rights of adults (other than age-restricted activities). They absolutely have the right to not have any information released to their parents without their written consent.

If you have a moral dilemma by not including the parents in the evaluation or treatment of a minor for sexually transmitted diseases, substance abuse, contraception, etc., encourage the teen to agree to include one parent. If this is refused, you can either treat the person or make a referral to someone who is comfortable with the situation. As long as the treatment situation is not an emergency and you've made sure that someone else is available to the patient, you have satisfied your duty.

Other Third Party Liability

In your relationship with a patient, a duty may be established to a third party if advice is given to this person/agency, or the third party is somehow included in the treatment plan. Whether or not your actions established a duty (making you liable for a possible negligence action) is determined by a court. Examples of this liability are as follows:

> • In 1980, a woman was told by her internist that she had syphilis (from a lab result). The physician told her to tell her husband so he could be treated. Both spouses blamed each other for being unfaithful, which led to a divorce. Two years later, the lab informed the physician that there was an error. The doctor called the patient, and both she and her ex-husband were understandably peeved. The husband then brought suit against the doctor, the lab company, etc.

In this case, duty was established because the physician advised the patient to tell the husband. It is easy to extrapolate from this case to some of the potential minefields present in everyday practice.

> • In 1993, a man from Tennessee died from a non-infectious disease (Rocky Mountain Spotted Fever). His wife subsequently died as well, and an action was brought against the doctor. The court stated the physician had a duty to warn the wife that she was at risk because the ticks that transmit the disease "tend to cluster." There are not a lot of "clustering ticks" sort of cases, but beware. It does make one speculate about how absurd things can become.

Remember, that to have a successful negligence suit, all four elements – duty, breach (dereliction), direct (proximate) cause, and damage – all must be satisfied. The controversial element in third party liability suits is that of duty. In the cases where there is the risk of violence, state statutes establish the presence of duty (in many cases). In the two cases discussed above, there are no pertinent statutes that would have clearly established a duty to a third party.

"Mrs. Nocturia, please sign this form which states that I warned you of the risk of tripping over the bedpost when you get up at night – just like your husband did."

Duties to Non-Identifiable Third Parties

These duties vary by state, but generally you can address your duty to non-identifiable third parties by warning the patient. These considerations include any illness or medication that may affect a patient's ability to drive safely, discovery of a genetic disorder that could affect other family members, use of medications under hazardous conditions, etc.

For example, consider a situation where you prescribe a medication that may be sedating. You would advise the patient that it may make him drowsy, and therefore he shouldn't drive after taking it. You then document that you explained the possible hazards to the patient. If he uses poor judgment and drives, and causes an accident where someone is injured, the patient is the culpable party. You are not liable for prescribing a sedating medication. The only catch would occur if the patient was not competent to understand your instructions.

Privilege

Unlike confidentiality, (which is again, the Clinician's Obligation, privilege belongs to the patient (the Patient's Right). If a patient exerts her privilege, this prevents the physician from disclosing any information obtained during the course of evaluation and treatment.

Privilege usually becomes an issue during litigation or in other legal settings. This is not something that physicians are involved with during day-to-day practice. It is incorrect to say that you can't divulge information about a patient because it is privileged (again, privilege belongs to the patient). If the patient was not available to make a decision regarding the release of information, and it was your belief that releasing information would be harmful, you can consider invoking privilege on the patient's behalf (through your lawyer).

Subpoenas

Most physicians at some point in their practice will receive a subpoena related to a patient's litigation (hopefully not against you). A subpoena may be served in person, or can be sent as a regular letter. The subpoena will state exactly what is required (usually that you, the physician, release a medical record to the court or appear in court). What next? As with anything legal, notify your lawyer.

Caveat

It is advisable to have a lawyer that you can contact with day-to-day questions in addition to the one your insurance company assigns if you are named in a malpractice suit. Your personal lawyer should be knowledgeable in all aspects of medical negligence and in the other legal problems a physician can face (intentional torts, administrative hearings, etc.). This individual has a primary duty to you, not to the health care organization or the insurance company.

Many physicians are confused about their duty regarding the confidentiality of medical records after being served with a subpoena. Must one respond and provide everything requested in a subpoena? Yes, and no. You have a legal duty to respond to the subpoena, but you don't necessarily have to do what the subpoena states, nor should you in many cases. A subpoena is issued when a judge agrees that the information requested by an attorney could reasonably be considered pertinent in a lawsuit. A subpoena is different (and on a lower level) than a court order. Here is one way to proceed upon receiving a subpoena:

1. Notify your attorney and your insurance company.

2. Contact the patient and request that he or she sign a release of information form authorizing the release of the information requested. When patients take legal action against someone, it is often their attorney who requests the information, and it is not usually a problem to obtain consent for the release of information.

3. If the patient refuses to authorize the release of information or doesn't answer your request, you can then respond to the subpoena by stating that the patient may want to exercise his or her privilege, and the court needs to decide if it wishes to override this. You must respond to a subpoena. After you submit your request to the court, the judge will then either cancel the

subpoena or direct you to provide the information through a court order.

4. If you receive a court order, you *must* respond. Failing to release information can bring a charge of contempt of court, leading to a possible fine or imprisonment.

A variation in this process that you may encounter is a *subpoena duces tecum*, which is a subpoena to report in person at a certain time and place, and to bring specific information with you (usually a medical record). When you appear with the record (or other information requested), you do not need to actually turn over the information unless ordered by the court. The mistake some physicians make is that they hand over the record to the first person who requests it without checking to see if this person actually has the authority to receive the information. Unfortunately, there are some lawyers who take advantage of inexperienced physicians. Again, it is imperative that you obtain legal counsel as soon as you receive a subpoena.

End of Life Issues

An area that has received an increasing amount of attention has been the rights of individuals (and their families) when death is near or imminent. Several of the important issues in this area are:

- The Right to Die
- Physician-Assisted Suicide
- Advanced Directives/Durable Powers of Attorney
- Hospice
- Ethics Committees

End of life issues are an area of medicine with many ethical and legal considerations. Many ethicists who write in this area may overestimate the level of understanding that an average physician has regarding these issues. It is crucial to be aware of which aspects fall on the ethical "slippery slope." Many doctors have conservative views on end of life issues, often based on fears of litigation.

The Right to Die

Much has been written about one of the most basic issues involving self-determination, the right to die. Supreme Court decisions have (almost) sanctioned this as a constitutional right, because this concept can be considered an extension of the right to refuse treatment (which is a constitutionally-protected right).

The major focus in end of life issues is generally on the right of competent individuals to refuse even life-sustaining treatment. The decisions of legal cases and legislation in all states support the autonomy of competent individuals to direct their medical care.

Is There a Difference Between Withholding and Withdrawing Life-Sustaining Treatment?

This issue is frequently brought to ethics committees, and is generally an issue such as, "Mrs. Smith was supposed to be a 'no-code,' but she ended up on the respirator and now we can't take her off. What should we do now?"

These cases are similar to the right to refuse treatment situations, although many physicians have trouble looking at it from this perspective. The dilemma appears to involve situations where a patient expresses a desire to halt life-sustaining treatment already in progress. Many clinicians believe there is a large difference between stopping treatment that has begun, and not starting treatment in the first place. This is not so. In situations involving competent individuals, or incompetent individuals who have clearly communicated their wishes through living wills (or have surrogate decision makers for healthcare decisions), the process is straight-forward.

Caveat

There is no difference, ethically or legally, between not starting and stopping a life-prolonging treatment. It can be helpful to look at this concept in reverse. If there was a difference, and in some way it was more legally or ethically risky to stop a life-prolonging treatment, rather than not start one, physicians might be less likely to initiate treatment.

Pragmatically and legally, there is no difference between acts and omissions that have the same outcome. As the court said in the *In Conroy* case: *"Whether necessary treatment is withheld at the outset or withdrawn later on, the consequence – the patient's death – is the same."*

A typical treatment algorithm recommended by ethicists (and lawyers) for **Do Not Resuscitate (DNR)** orders reads as follows:

If the patient with a terminal condition does not desire to be intubated and everyone agrees it would not reverse the condition, then everyone is usually comfortable not initiating treatment. But, if there is a disagreement between either the family and patient or physician, then the patient can be intubated while the situation and decision is re-evaluated. If there was the fear that once intubated – always intubated, the decisions would become harder.

For elderly patients who have a condition that will likely cause death within a period of time, there is usually support for the wishes of patients who have advanced directives stating the patient's wishes for life-saving measures. The concept of "futility" is widely discussed in the literature, but is not a useful term operationally because it lacks a clear, legal definition. Most physicians and staff providing care to patients with terminal conditions use the term to mean that treatment is unlikely to restore health or quality of life, and that it will accomplish little more than allowing the person a brief extension of life.

An ethically difficult case might involve a patient with end-stage cancer who refuses to make an advanced directive, and who arrives in the emergency room already having been intubated by the EMTs. In this situation, the patient's family and physician can usually provide guidance on how to proceed.

Another difficult situation is sometimes termed "The Daughter From California." This scenario has both the person's family and the treatment team in agreement that life support should be stopped. However, the long-estranged daughter arrives (and as Murphy's Law would have it, is usually a physician or a lawyer), refuses to give permission, and threatens to sue the hospital if mom or dad is taken off of life support. The best way to handle any difficult case is to involve a member of the institution's ethics committee.

More Tough Cases

- A Jehovah's Witness patient who will die without a transfusion

- A quadriplegic patient on a respirator who wants it turned off

- A teenager in a chronic vegetative state whose family wants to cease enteral feedings

These are some of the cases that go to the courts, where the following factors are considered:

The individual's rights and autonomy
vs.
The state's interests:
- do no harm
- ensuring the ethical bases in clinical practice are followed
- the duty to prevent suicide
- preserving life
- innocent third parties should be protected

The courts generally tend to support the right of a competent patient to refuse or stop treatment, even if it is life sustaining. This is applied particularly if the patient has a terminal illness, has a diminished quality of life with minimal hope of improvement, or if the treatment itself can be difficult to endure.

Two of the most important right to refuse treatment/right to die cases are those of *In re. Quinlan* (1976) and *Cruzan v. Director* (1990). Both cases revolved around the wishes of the family to discontinue life-sustaining treatment for their daughters. The major issue centered around trying to determine what the patient would have chosen if she had been competent to make the decision.

The *Cruzan* court found that each person's decision to refuse consent to any invasive act (including the delivery of food and water) was constitutionally protected. However, in this case, the court supported the state's right to require evidence as to the wishes of the incompetent person (at the standard of *clear and convincing evidence*).

Most courts do not lump hydration and artificial nutrition in with comfort care – they consider it a life-sustaining medical treatment, which can be refused like any other treatment.

Advance Directives

An **advance directive** is a process which allows a person to extend their decision-making autonomy from the present to a time when they may become incompetent to make their own treatment decisions. All 50 states have statutes authorizing some form of advance directive. Forty-six states allow both a living will and durable powers of attorney for healthcare.

Part of the 1990 Patient Self Determination Act was to require healthcare institutions to provide written information to patients at the time of admission regarding their right to refuse treatment, and their right to establish an advance directive. Every state makes available to patients a form for executing an advance directive. These forms are in all hospitals, and several books have been published to guide patients through this process.

Caveat
An advance directive that is legal in one state may not be in another. Attempts are being made to ensure that all states will recognize the person's expressed wishes, but if you have a patient from New York who spends the winter in Florida, you may want to advise them to check on whether their advance directive will be respected in a particular state.

Physician-Assisted Suicide
Proponents of **physician-assisted suicide (PAS)** have advocated this act for patients with terminal illnesses who are in severe pain. The AMA and several other organizations have decreed that assisted suicide is not compatible with the healing role of physicians. What these organizations do advocate is careful attention to the needs of the patient – addressing both better pain management and palliative care.

What Is PAS?
PAS involves physicians *assisting* in the dying process. This needs to be distinguished morally, ethically, and legally from **euthanasia**, which is directly causing another person's death.

The increase in activism by both patients and physicians led to the Oregon Death With Dignity Act of 1996.

Patients and their physicians have challenged state laws prohibiting physician-assisted suicide. Most notable are the two cases reviewed by the U.S. Supreme Court in 1997, which did not rule on the issue of PAS, but rather did not agree that a person has a constitutionally protected right to kill himself.

- *Washington v. Glucksberg* involved a lawsuit initiated by several patients and their doctors who challenged state bans that violated their due process liberty interest under the 14th Amendment.

- In *Vacco v. Quill*, there was a challenge to the New York law prohibiting PAS. The claim was that the law violated the 14th amendment equal protection clause for those desiring PAS.

The Supreme Court found that neither case involved a violation of any constitutional right. This finding did not, per se, prohibit any state from passing a law allowing PAS, but stated that challenges on the above grounds were not valid. What the Supreme Court clearly took a stand on was that physicians have a duty to aggressively manage a terminally ill patient's pain:

"It is widely recognized that the provision of pain medication is ethically and professionally acceptable, even when the treatment may hasten the patients' death, if the medication is intended to alleviate pain and severe discomfort, not to cause death."

And from Justice O'Connor:

"A patient who is suffering from a terminal illness and who is experiencing great pain has no legal barriers to obtaining medication from qualified physicians, even to the point of causing unconsciousness and hastening death."

What has been an undisputed positive outcome of the Right to Die/PAS debate is the advancement of education and knowledge about pain management, and the treatment of depression in terminally ill patients. Dialogue has been enhanced in many forums.

There have also been several papers published with guidelines on how to handle requests for PAS and treat the terminally ill.

One author (Singer, 1999) identified the following points for enhancing the quality of care at the end of life:

- Receiving adequate pain and symptom management
- Avoiding inappropriate prolongation of dying
- Achieving a sense of control
- Relieving burdens
- Strengthening relationships with loved ones

End of life duties to patients are increasingly recognized as ethical obligations.

At the time of writing, one hotly debated issue is the bill proposed to Congress called the Pain Relief Promotion Act of 1999. Although this bill is superficially worded to offer legal protection for physicians who provide palliative care, it may well cause physicians already hesitant to provide adequate pain relief to become more conservative. This bill was meant to override the Oregon PAS law, and has provisions for criminally punishing physicians who use controlled substances to cause a patients death. One of the primary concerns is that DEA agents would determine if a medical treatment was appropriate.

Ethics Committees

Every organization should have a mechanism by which ethical concerns can be addressed. A hospital will have a formal **Institutional Ethics Committee (IEC)** with a membership that usually includes the following: physicians (primary care, intensivist, psychiatrist), risk manager, nurse, lawyer, chaplain, administrator, social worker, and other members the group deems appropriate. More important than the titles or positions of the committee members are personal characteristics: ethical assessment skills, process skills, and interpersonal skills.

This is not the type of committee to which members should be under duress to join – participation should be voluntary.

The IEC members will be adept at dealing with the various ethical issues that arise in an organization, and which commonly involve end-of-life matters. Even organizations without a formal committee (usually smaller ambulatory care practices) should have a process in place to address the issues that do arise. The American Society for Bioethics and Humanities, or other similar organizations, can provide additional guidance.

Hospice

Hospice programs offer the terminally ill the best opportunity to exercise their autonomy, and maintain their dignity at the end of life. Hospice care is interdisciplinary, provides support to the entire family, and is much better positioned to provide the appropriate care to the dying through palliation of their symptoms.

Few would argue that a person enrolled in a hospice program has a better exposure to medical professionals who are knowledgeable about pain management, palliative care, and are comfortable with the legal and ethical issues surrounding end-of-life decisions. Unfortunately, only a small number of individuals who could benefit greatly from a hospice program use this opportunity.

A large part of this problem can be explained by the difficulty in making accurate medical prognoses. For patients to be eligible to receive hospice care under the Medicare Hospice Benefit, their physicians must certify that the person is terminally ill, and has a life expectancy of six months or less. Up to 50% of those who are terminally ill in the U.S. are not offered the opportunity for hospice enrollment. The majority of those entering hospices have made the decision so late that they may only have one or two months left to live.

Some physicians are unaware of the range of services hospices offer. Others are averse to telling patients about their terminal status (due to a concern over the patient's fragility, or their own discomfort). Physicians may think of hospice care only for cancer or AIDS patients, when there are patients with many terminal conditions who could benefit greatly from these programs. Some physicians are also reluctant to prescribe the palliative care recommended by hospice medical staff because it focuses on symptom improvement only, not treating the underlying disease.

Physicians trained in palliative care focus on alleviating suffering instead of the prolongation of life without quality. Pain management is performed effectively. Parenteral fluids or enteral nutrition is rarely recommended. These interventions are made only when an identified symptom can clearly be improved. Some physicians are uncomfortable unless they can provide all possible treatments for patients (even those who are agreeable to DNR orders).

Hospice care will ensure that patients and their families understand the levels of available care. Staff will prepare family members for the day when the patient develops respiratory distress. This may include which papers, medic alert tags, etc. to have handy so that if an emergency response team (911) is called, they will be informed about the patient's living will and DNR request.

If you are ethically committed to preserving a patient's dignity throughout his lifespan, an awareness of, and involvement with, hospice programs is essential. Failure to discuss the palliative care options, and particularly failure to properly manage pain, may result in a legal action against you, though these issues are perhaps more ethical in nature. Recently, a state board of medicine took formal action against a physician who under-treated several patients in need of aggressive pain management.

Boundary Issues

Boundary issues can be divided into two varieties – **boundary**

violations and **boundary crossings**. These terms originate from mental health parlance, and describe a spectrum of behaviors ranging from marginally inappropriate behavior to the clearly inappropriate relationships that occur between doctors and patients. This spectrum runs from mildly ill-advised actions to those that may result in felony convictions.

Boundary Crossings
Boundary "crossings" are minimal transgressions of the ethical guidelines which address the DPR. Such boundaries are established to ensure that there is not even the perception that a physician has breached the strict fiduciary responsibilities of trust and confidence, and never puts personal interests ahead of those of the patient.

Boundary issues are most strongly emphasized in mental health care, but are certainly applicable to all physicians. The more conservative physicians are, the less likely they are to find themselves in legal difficulty. Some of the healthiest risk management attitudes and behaviors you can have toward your patients include:

Do not become involved in personal relationships with patients
Avoid the following activities with patients: going out for lunch, having a drink, entering into business relationships, having them to your house, giving or accepting gifts (other than those with limited value). Now, of course common sense must apply – if you live in a small town and the majority of the citizens are your patients, it is unrealistic to expect that you will not establish some type of relationship with them.

Never share personal information with a patient
This intimates a friendship instead of a professional relationship.

Don't touch patients except to perform a physical examination
Again, use common sense. A hand on a shoulder for encouragement, or holding a dying patient's hand is not what this recommendation advises against. While *you* might see a hug as being entirely nonsexual and merely supportive, the patient may not.

Don't make exceptions in your schedule for select patients
Don't agree to see only certain patients after hours – this is frequently a prelude to a boundary violation.

Don't set different fees for different patients
This practice is not advised unless it is based on a patient's ability to pay, and is then applied to everyone in a particular income category. Waiving the co-pay or giving professional courtesy may actually be a violation of state or federal regulations.

Maintain a stance of neutrality
Provide quality care, demonstrate empathy with your patients, and offer support for the decisions they make as competent and autonomous individuals. Don't give advice or tell them what they "should" do (other than the obvious things like stop smoking, get more exercise, buckle up, etc.). Do not recommend they get a divorce, quit their job, or sue their mother!

Are boundary crossings ever acceptable? At times, yes. Some examples are:

- Giving an elderly patient a ride home on an icy day

- Sending a card expressing condolences over a family member's death

- Sending a gift, or attending the wedding of your patient's only child

These situations are examples of ones in which you are clearly putting the best interests or safety of your patient first, and would not be misconstrued.

Boundary Violations

The majority of boundary violations begin quite innocently. Drs. Simon and Gutheil note that for mental health professionals, most boundary violations begin "between the chair and the door," when the physician lets her guard down with idle chit-chat. The most serious of all boundary violations, and the one having the greatest impact upon the practitioner and patient, is having sexual relationships with patients.

Caveat

Never have a sexual relationship with a patient. This is the number one boundary violation that can cause you to lose the farm – or, at the least, your medical license. The prohibition of physician's sexual contact with patients dates back to the Hippocratic Oath:

"I will come for the benefit of the sick, remaining free of all intentional injustice, of all mischief, and in particular of sexual relationships with both female and male persons, be they free or slaves."

For psychiatrists and other mental health professionals, having a sexual relationship with a current patient represents the gravest error in judgment possible. A psychiatrist having sex with a patient is committing a felony in at least fourteen states (at the time of writing). This number has been expanding in recent years. Minnesota has a mandatory reporting law (if a patient tells her current psychiatrist she had sex with her previous psychiatrist, the second psychiatrist must report this).

Legal restrictions on DPRs exist because one member (the patient) cannot make a free and competent choice. These laws stem from the same prohibition of sexual relations between adults and minors. Many of the state laws have language taken from prohibition of incest statutes.

It is also unethical and/or illegal for a mental health professional to have sex with a former patient (again, state statutes vary on this point). Many states have what is called a "perpetuity" rule, meaning that *once someone is a patient, he is always considered to be a patient.* The perpetuity rule has widespread support. It is difficult to justify, that in a specified period of time, that the power imbalance in a therapeutic relationship will change. Physicians are put in special positions of trust and confidence.

There are also practical issues involved. Ask any lawyer if a problem exists in becoming romantically involved with former patients, and the smart response will be "*Not if you live happily ever after.*" If you marry a former patient and don't live happily ever after, your soon-to-be ex-spouse may well claim that you took advantage of her vulnerable position as a patient. In addition to the divorce settlement, you may be sued for a variety of things, as well as being reported to your state board of medicine.

A not infrequent dynamic is that a patient interested in pursuing a relationship with her physician may go through an initial period of idealization. All goes well until the physician does something the patient doesn't like (such as trying to end the relationship). This brings about a very potent devaluation, which can lead to many personal and professional problems, including a lawsuit.

One self-report survey of physicians who admitted to having sex with one or more patients during their careers revealed the following:

- All primary care physicians   10%
- Obstetrician-gynecologists   18%
- Psychiatrists   5%

This information, and the fact that having sex with a patient currently under your care is grounds for action to remove your license, is reason to take heed. Most specialty societies are currently discussing this issue in their ethics divisions. While there is no debate on the ethical transgression of having sex with current patients, there is considerable discussion about establishing guidelines regarding former patients.

In a successful 1998 lawsuit against a healthcare professional for having sex with a patient, the court held that: "*If a medical professional not practicing in the field of mental health enters into a relationship of trust and confidence with a patient, and offers counseling on personal matters to that patient, this is*

*taking on a role similar to that of a psychiatrist or psychologist,
and that professional should be bound by the* same *standards
as would bind a psychiatrist or psychologist in a similar situation."*

Using this reasoning, it is easy to see where a lawyer will attempt
to hold all physicians to the standard to which psychiatrists are
held (that sexual relationships are illegal, not just unethical).
Family physicians prescribe more fluoxetine in the U.S. than
do psychiatrists. As is appropriate in many cases, the primary
care provider treats patients for depression or anxiety disorders.
Once a psychiatric diagnosis is made, and treatment is provided
(e.g. "supportive psychotherapy"), primary care providers may
well be held to the psychiatric standard if they have sexual
relationships with patients.

Caveat

Several profiles have been compiled of physicians at risk for
sexual misconduct. Some of these features are: male, ages 40
– 50, marital discord, and alcohol abuse/dependence. The
majority of physicians who were charged with sexual impropriety
(and lost their licenses or received prison sentences) did not
believe they were at risk for having sexual relationships with
patients.

Usually there is a progression of boundary crossing along a
slippery slope of unethical behavior. At some point the
acceptable doctor-patient boundary is breached, and this
eventually progresses to a sexual relationship. This process
can begin by calling a patient by her first name, or accepting a
gift. . . then running into her after work and sharing a drink. . .
then offering her a ride home, agreeing to see her in the evening
when the staff have gone home. . .

The safest guideline is to limit your relationship with any patient
to one of professional intent only. You want to avoid any
speculation about your ability to be completely objective in your
role as a physician.

Standby

A **standby** is a person who is present during a medical exam. Any organization accredited by JCAHO must have policies in place regarding standbys. The patient has the right to request a standby of the same sex, and the physician has the right to refuse to do a physical exam if a standby is not present.

It is always prudent to have a standby present when examining a patient's breasts or genitals. The presence of a standby should be offered even when the physician and patient are of the same sex. Standby personnel should be present at any time you feel uncomfortable with a patient – from outright flirtatiousness to situations where you just have a gut feeling something isn't right.

The patient should always have the opportunity to request a standby. Your policy should be prominently displayed in your office, and can be part of the posted patient rights and responsibilities.

Caveat

Do not use a patient's spouse or friend as the standby, even if it is more convenient than using one of your staff. If a standby was present for an examination, add her name to the medical record.

Dual Relationships With Patients

This section covers any relationship a doctor has outside of a typical DPR. The guiding principle here is the same as for sexual relationships with patients. . . don't get involved in these situations. Examples of ill-advised dual relationships, even for non-psychiatric physicians, are:

Developing a close friendship with a patient
There are many pitfalls to this, the least of which involves confidentiality issues (particularly if mandatory reporting is

involved). Any relationship presents a potential conflict of interest. Patients often develop an expectation for special treatment. This doesn't mean that you must decline all party invitations if you live in a small town and many of the community members are your patients.

Involvement in any business proposition with a patient
If there is an unfavorable outcome from this venture, the patient can sue you saying she felt coerced and that her medical care might have suffered if she didn't go along with your suggestions.

In many instances, physicians get into trouble because they are trying to be helpful. Provide your help and support as a physician by practicing the highest quality of medical care possible, not as a friend or business partner. More information about this topic is provided in Chapter 10.

Abandonment

Many clinicians believe that once they have established a relationship with a patient, it cannot be put asunder. Physicians who believe this will be pleasantly surprised that our system truly does support the rights of all parties – doctors included.

Once you have established a duty to a patient, you do have one absolute responsibility, which is to provide that patient with the SOC for his evaluation and treatment. You are not compelled to continue this relationship when it is not in the best interest of either party. There are a variety of situations when it is perfectly appropriate for you to consider terminating a DPR.

Remember that there is only one absolute – *After establishing a duty to a patient, you must provide care in emergency situations and offer alternative treatment options for that patient.*

Physicians become liable for charges of abandonment if they do not meet the above criteria. Remember, that intentional torts are not usually covered by malpractice insurance coverage.

Some of the more appropriate reasons to terminate a DPR are as follows:

- The course of treatment is completed (this is the most common reason)

- You are retiring or moving

- The patient exhibits continued noncompliance with medical treatment

- The patient has engaged in repeated harassment of you or your staff

- The patient engages in persistent seductive behavior

- The patient is not being honest about medical matters

In each case, the patient must be provided with written notification that you are withdrawing from her care. If at all possible, discuss this on the last scheduled visit or send a letter.

Caveat

In every case, send a letter via certified mail with a return receipt requested. The letter should state (at the minimum):

- That you are no longer going to continue providing medical care

- The reasons why care is being withdrawn; this is not necessary in all cases, but is recommended if the reasons are not likely to be inflammatory

- State that you will provide any needed care for a short period of time while he finds another physician (usually 30 days)

- List alternatives for care, and include names and phone numbers

- Outline what the patient should do in case of an emergency

It is strongly recommended that you review your "generic" letter with your attorney.

Good Samaritan Laws

Every state has a Good Samaritan Statute (in some form) that applies to those who respond to the scene of an emergency. The details vary, but all provide some form of immunity from claims of negligence for those who render aid in an emergency without a specific duty to do so. These statutes are in place to encourage physicians (and others) to assist in an emergency, without incurring legal risks. While physicians are encouraged to assist in emergencies, there is no (legal) duty to do so. Once a physician stops at the scene, she needs to remain there until help arrives (of an equal or greater ability to assist).

Interestingly, there are a few cases where these statutes have been applied to an emergency which occurs within a healthcare facility. A well-known case in this regard involved an obstetrician who was in a hospital when a "code blue" was announced. He was the only physician present, and administered a benzodiazepine to a woman having seizures. She died from subsequent respiratory arrest. The court found for the defendant physician, and opined that this physician had no duty to the patient. She was not his patient, he was not providing on-call coverage for the service, nor was he a member of the code team. Check your state law for the exact applicability.

Closing the gap in the liability coverage of physicians responding to an emergency occurred when the **Aviation Medical Assistance Act of 1998** was passed. As part of this law, there is Good Samaritan liability language which protects any healthcare provider who is "licensed, certified, or otherwise

qualified to provide medical care in a state," and renders care in good faith to ill or injured passengers during the flight. The wording reads: "*An individual shall not be liable for damages in any action brought in a federal or state court arising from an act or omission of the individual in providing or attempting to provide assistance in the case of an in-flight medical emergency.*"

There is also a proposal recommending the appropriate use of automatic external defibrillators on aircraft, which was the primary reason for this bill.

References

APA Guidelines on Confidentiality.
American Psychiatric Association, Washington D.C., 1987

Appelbaum PS, Grisso T: **Assessing Patients' Capacities to Consent to Treatment**.
NEJM 319:1635-1638, 1988

Appelbaum PS, Grisso T: **Capacities of Hospitalized, Medically Ill Patients to Consent to Treatment**.
Psychosomatics 38:119-125, 1997

Appelbaum PS, Jorgenson LM, Sutherland PK: **Sexual Relationships Between Physicians and Patients**.
Arch Intern Med 154:2561-2565, 1994

Arie T: **Some Legal Aspects of Mental Capacity**.
BMJ 313:156-158, 1996

Aviation Medical Assistance Act, Public Law 105-170, 1998

Block S, Billings A: **Patients' Requests to Hasten Death**.
Arch Intern Med 154:2039-2047, 1994

Bradshaw v. Daniel, 854 S.W.2d 865 (Tenn.1993)

Bursztajn HJ, Harding HP, Gutheil TG, et al: **Beyond Cognition: The Role of Disordered Affective States in Impairing Competence to Consent to Treatment**.
Bull Am Acad Psychiatry Law 19:383-388, 1991

Cady RF: **The Legal Forum**.
JONA's Healthcare Law, Ethics, and Reg 1:9-11, 1999

Campbell ML: **The Oath: An Investigation of the Injunction Prohibiting Physician-Patient Sexual Relations**.
Perspect Biol Med 32:300-309, 1998

Canterbury v. Spence, 464 F 2d 772 (1972)

Christensen K, Haroun A, Schneiderman LJ et al: **Decision-Making Capacity for Informed Consent in the Older Population**.
Bull Am Acad Psych Law 23:353-365

Code of Medical Ethics – Current Opinions with Annotations.
American Medical Association, Chicago, 1999

Cruzan v. Director, Missouri Dept of Health. 497 U.S. 261, 1990

Doyal L: **Informed Consent in Medical Research**.
BMJ 314:1107-1111, 1997

Emanuel EJ, Danies ER, Fairclough DL, et al: **The Practice of Euthanasia and Physician-Assisted Suicide in the U.S.: Adherence to Proposed Safeguards and Effects on Physicians**.
JAMA 280:507-513, 1998

Emanuel LL: **Facing Requests for Physician-Assisted Suicide – Toward a Practical Principled Clinical Skill Set**.
JAMA 280:643-647, 1998

Emanuel LL, Emanuel EJ, Stoeckle JD, et al: **Advanced Directives: Stability of Patients' Treatment Choices**.
Arch Intern Med 154:209, 217, 1994

Fitten LJ, Waite MS: **Impact of Medical Hospitalization on Treatment Decision-Making Capacity in the Elderly**.
Arch Intern Med 150:1717-1721, 1990

Forensic Psychiatry Review Course Handbook.
American Academy of Psychiatry and the Law, 1997

Foubister V: **More Centers Cited for Ethics Lapses in Research**.
AMA News 42(41):8,10, 1999

Foubister V: **Oregon Doctor Cited for Negligence for Undertreated Pain**.
AMA News 42(45):7, 9, 1999

Gostin LO: **Deciding Life and Death in the Courtroom. From Quinlan to Cruzan, Glucksberg, and Vacco – A Brief History and Analysis of Constitutional Protection of the "Right to Die."**
JAMA 278:1523-1528, 1999

Grisso T, Appelbaum PS: *Assessing Competence to Consent to Treatment.*
Oxford University Press, New York, 1998

Grisso T, Appelbaum PS: **The MacArthur Treatment Competence Study – III: Abilities of Patients to Consent to Psychiatric and Medical Treatments**.
Law Human Behav 19:149-174, 1995

Gutheil TG, Bursztajn HJ, Brodsky A: **Malpractice Prevention Through the Sharing of Uncertainty: Informed Consent and the Therapeutic Alliance**.
NEJM 311:49-51, 1984

Gutheil TG, Simon RI: **Between the Chair and the Door: Boundary Issues in the Therapeutic Transition Zone**.
Harvard Review of Psychiatry 2:336-340, 1995

Harty-Golder BH: **Protect Patient, Self When Reporting Abuse**.
Florida Medical Business 12(22):7, 1999

In re Conroy, 486 A2d 1209 (NJ 1985)

In re Quinlan, 355 A2d 647(NJ), cert. denied, 429 US922 (1976)

Johnson SH: **Judicial Review of Disciplinary Action for Sexual Misconduct in the Practice of Medicine**.
JAMA 270:1596, 1993

Katz M, Abbey S, Rydall A et al: **Psychiatric Consultation for Competency to Refuse Medical Treatment – A Retrospective Study of Patient Characteristics and Outcome**.
Psychosomatics 36:33-41, 1995

Knowles FE, Liberto J, Baker FM et al: **Competency Evaluations in a VA Hospital – A 10-year Perspective**.
Gen Hosp Psychiatry 16:119-124, 1994

Marson DC, McInturff B, Hawkings L et al: **Consistency of Physician Judgment of Capacity to Consent in Mild Alzheimer's Disease**.
J Am Geriatr Soc 45:453-457, 1997

Marta M: **Genetic Testing: Do Healthcare Professionals Have a Duty to Tell a Patient's Family Member that They May Be at Risk?**
J of Healthcare Risk Management 19:26-38, 1999

McCracken v. Walls, Kaufman 717 A.2d 346(D.C. 1998)

McKinnon K, Cournos F, Stanley B: **Rivers in Practice: Clinicians' Assessments of Patients' Decision-Making Capacity**.
Hosp Community Psychiatry 40:1159-1162, 1989

Miller FG, Quill TE, Brody H, et al: **Regulating Physician-Assisted Death**.
NEJM 331:119-123, 1994

Molien v. Kaiser Foundation Hospitals [27 Cal.3d 916] 1980

Natanson v. Kline, 350 P.2d 1093 (Kansas 1960)

Nelson WA: **Evaluating Your Ethics Committee**.
Healthcare Executive 51(1):48-49

Orentlicher D: **Must CPR Be An Issue in Futile Situations?**
AM News 42:9-10, Sept 6, 1999

Pain Relief Promotion Act of 1999. HR 2260

Patient Self-Determination Act of 1990
42 United States Code Sections 1395, 1396

Roush S, Virkhead G, Koo D, et al: **Mandatory Reporting of Diseases and Conditions by Health Care Professionals and Laboratories**.
JAMA 282:164-170, 1999

Rozovsky FA: **When Does "No Mean No" in the Emergency Department?**
The Rozovsky Group, Inc.
www.therozovskygroup.com, reviewed 10/12/99

Schneiderman N: **Relationship of Advance Directives to Physician-Patient Communication**.
Arch Intern Med 154:909-913, 1994

Scholoendorff v. Society of New York Hospitals, 211 N.Y. 125 (1914)

Searight HR, Campbell DC: **Physician-Patient Sexual Contact: Ethical and Legal Issues and Clinical Guidelines**.
J Fam Pract 36:647-653, 1993

Shore D: **Ethical Principles and Informed Consent: An NIMH Perspective**.
Psychpharmacology Bulletin 32:7-10, 1996

Simon R: **Boundary Violations in Psychotherapy**.
The Mental Health Practitioner and the Law., Ed. Lifson LE and Simon RI.
Harvard Univ Press, Cambridge, 1998

Singer PA, Martin DK, Kelner M: **Quality End-of-Life Care**.
JAMA 281:163-168, 1999

Solomon M: **Decisions Near the End of Life: Professional Views on Life-Sustaining Treatments**.
Am J Public Health 83:14-20, 1993

Steinbrook R, Lo B: **Artificial Feeding – Solid Ground, Not a Slippery Slope**.
NEJM 318:286-290, 1988

Sullivan MD, Youngner SJ: **Depression, Competence and the Right to Refuse Lifesaving Medical Treatment**.
Am J Psychiatry 151:971-978, 1994

Tarasoff v. Regents, CA Supr. Ct (1976) 70, 71, 232

Vacco v. Quill, 117 S. Ct 2293, 1997

Washington v. Glucksberg, 117 S. Ct 2258, 1997

5. Limiting Liability

A long habit of not thinking a thing wrong, gives it a superficial appearance of being right.

Thomas Paine, *Common Sense*

Communication

Developing superior communication skills is crucial for physicians who want to improve their "art of medicine" abilities and take effective steps in limiting their legal liability.

Factoids on Communication

• A finding frequently quoted in training seminars is that during routine patient visits, doctors interrupted and redirected their patients within 18 seconds. This immediately sets the stage for patients to feel ignored and patronized.

• Another study demonstrated that although physicians solicited their patients' concerns in 75% of the cases, patients were able to complete their initial statements only 28% of the time, and were redirected after only 23 seconds. When patients were allowed to complete their full communication, they needed on average only 6 additional seconds!

• Thirty-five percent of the patients who were redirected during interviews raised additional concerns at the end of the evaluation, compared to only 15% of the patients who were able to complete their initial statements.

• In a survey of physicians who had not been the subject of a lawsuit, the majority credited rapport, good communication, and compassion for patients as the reasons they had been able to stay out of court. Only 14% credited their good medical skills.

Communication can be enhanced without necessarily spending more time with patients. This is accomplished by maximizing the efficiency of their visits. Suggestions for increasing efficiency are as follows:

Patients Who Are Followed for a Chronic Disease

A key recommendation is to tell patients to keep a list of their questions. It can be helpful to tell them ahead of time that you may not have the chance to discuss all of their concerns, but you are interested in knowing what bothers them the most. By simply asking about their principal concerns, you convey a strong sense of genuinely caring for your patients' welfare.

For Initial Evaluations

It can be very helpful to develop a questionnaire that centers on your area of expertise, but that also covers peripheral areas. Examples of the latter are: domestic abuse, tobacco use (not just cigarettes), alcohol use, allergies, and a list of all medications (including vitamins, nutritional supplements, herbal medicines, etc.). An appropriately trained assistant can review the questionnaire, clarify the information provided, and begin health promotion and education (e.g. tobacco cessation). Patients could then watch videotapes geared towards their particular education needs – all while waiting to see you.

One of the main reasons patients dislike visiting physicians is that they are kept waiting without an explanation. A helpful guideline is the "Twenty Minute Rule." This involves having a staff member inform patients about the reason for any delay, and the approximate additional wait within 20 minutes of the scheduled appointment. An apology for the delay goes a long way towards ensuring patient satisfaction. If delays aren't acknowledged, patients feel that their time is not considered to be valuable.

Consider the situation where someone who is an established patient of your practice leaves because he was not seen in a timely fashion. If a follow-up appointment is not arranged, and something happens because he wasn't assessed, you may well be liable, even though it was the patient who left. This is based on your duty to, and abandonment of, the patient.

If that same patient storms out the door on several occasions and is rude to your staff, it may well be time to arrange for someone else to take over that person's care using the stepwise approach noted on pages 114-115.

Documentation

Good documentation is crucial to good patient care. Even a physician with total recall for every patient's diagnosis, list of medications, lab values, dates of preventive actions, etc. can still get run over by a truck. Good charting practices allow everyone involved in the patient's care to share information, which enhances medical decision-making.

There are many state laws governing medical documentation. If your organization is assessed by the Joint Commission for Health Care Organizations, or the National Committee for Quality Assurance, medical record documentation is a major focus. Unfortunately, for many physicians, writing in the medical record takes a back seat to other patient care priorities.

Modified Nike® Caveat
Just do it, but simply.

There are many excellent references that provide guidelines for improving documentation. The process of improving documentation begins with your own critical review. Do your notes show that you discussed the diagnosis? Can your records provide evidence that IC was obtained for any treatment or procedure? Was the rationale for ongoing treatment explained, as well as the necessity for follow-up visits?

Ensure that your staff document their interactions with patients as well. Medical notes do not need to be lengthy, they just need to cover the essentials.

Stocking a complete set of patient education handouts is a great way of doing the most with a limited amount of time. You or your nurse can review the handout with the patient and answer any questions. If so, record these questions, and indicate that they were reviewed. If you use the same handouts consistently, you don't need to write a novel for each diagnosis, just document that you have provided and reviewed the handout with the patient.

Corrections to Medical Records

Changes can be made easily, quickly, and safely. Here are some rules to follow:

Changes Should "Stand Alone"

Anyone reviewing the medical record should be able to easily tell when, why, and who made any changes. Many physicians put a line through the original entry, and then initial and date the alteration. However, this doesn't satisfy the "stand alone" requirement. As an example, let's say you write an entry in another patient's chart. Put an 'X' through your note and write in the margin "Entry in wrong record," and then initial and date it. In the correct record, write a note stating "Entry for such-and-such date written in wrong record."

Do Not Obliterate Entries With Pens, Markers or White-Out

If the record is ever used in litigation, it will look like you did something wrong and were trying to hide this fact (even if it was something innocuous). A good lawyer will enlarge an obliterated entry to a disquieting four-foot by six-foot size and make it an exhibit. When jurors are bored by listening to medical testimony, their gaze will be drawn to this display.

Furthermore, the technology available today to date documents, papers, and inks is quite powerful. Do not try to "fix" a record if you are concerned about a lawsuit or have received a subpoena. Be honest. If there is proof that you intentionally tried to change a record to avoid blame, the lawsuit may now enter the realm of intentional tort (and remember, your insurance company won't pay for your defense). If there is evidence that a physician participated in a cover-up of some sort, the usual statute of limitations for negligence may not apply. Juries want to find for the defendant physician, and will accept honest mistakes. But they don't like liars.

Write Legibly

Poor handwriting can be the cause of a court decision against you. Physicians have a duty to write so those involved in a patient's care can read what has been said. Illegible progress notes can be a problem, but the greatest legal risk comes from unreadable treatment orders or prescriptions. If the proverbial "reasonable person" cannot decipher your hieroglyphics, it is quite likely that you will be hung out to dry.

Feelings of resentment can develop in those that must decipher the less-than-legible handwriting of doctors. Poor penmanship can be seen as stemming from arrogance, and those around you are subsequently less likely to be there to help you in the hundreds of subtle ways that can make your job easier.

Keep Personal Opinions About the Care Provided by Others Out of the Medical Record

Any concern you have about the care rendered to Mrs. Smithereen by another member of the treatment team should be discussed with that person (and addressed through your organization's RM process). The medical record is a legal document and may be fully discoverable in court. QA/RM documents are generally not discoverable, though in some jurisdictions judges may be allowed to review this information. If you are a consultant and have found that the patient's primary physician has prescribed a medication that you do not recommend, you can of course record this in your recommendations, and can add "Will discuss choice of meds with Dr. Lecter."

Caveat

If you make disparaging comments of any nature in the medical record, in addition to being inappropriate, you may well have freely provided full documentation in a defamation suit – against you! This, as you will no doubt recall, will *not* be covered by your malpractice insurance.

Make Certain Your Statements Aren't Ambiguous

Here are some gems. These bloopers have been collected from several sources, and are allegedly from actual medical records:

- "Patient evaluated by social worker found to be psychotic."
- "The patient refused an autopsy."
- "Patient had waffles for breakfast and anorexia for lunch."
- "She is numb from her toes down."
- "On the 2nd day the knee was better and on the 3rd day it disappeared completely."
- "Patient was alert and unresponsive."
- "The patient has been depressed ever since she began seeing me in 1993."
- "Rectal exam revealed a normal size thyroid."
- "Testicles are missing on this woman."
- "Patient has two teenage children but no other abnormalities."
- "Large brown stool ambulating in hall."
- "I saw your patient today who is still under our car for physical therapy."
- "She stated she has been constipated for most of her life, until she got a divorce."
- "If it weren't for the fact the patient is dead, I would say he was in perfect health."
- "Discharge status – alive but without permission."

Check your state laws to determine how long you need to keep medical records. The state will also indicate what should occur when you retire or die. If you conduct psychotherapy or provide perinatal care, it is prudent to keep your records forever (or at least a summary of them). You must have some provision in your will for who will become the guardian of your records.

Consultations

Requesting consultations from other physicians, on either a formal or informal basis, ensures that patients receive an appropriate level of care. Every state requires physicians to practice within their areas of expertise, and to provide a level of care that a similarly trained and experienced colleague would provide.

As Harry Callaghan (of Dirty Harry fame) said, "A man's gotta know his limitations." This applies even more so to physicians. The majority of medical practitioners are comfortable knowing when to ask for help or a second opinion. Unfortunately, those who don't ask for assistance are often the ones who need it the most.

Caveat

"Doubt is not a very pleasant condition, but certainty is absurd."

Voltaire

A valuable tool in your armamentarium of good patient care (and an asset in minimizing risk) is the informal or "curbside" consult. This term refers to a communication between colleagues where a clinical problem is succinctly presented and advice is sought for a specific point or two. Curbside consults are underused, and a win-win proposition. Many physicians are hesitant to offer curbside opinions because of their legal liability. This is largely an unfounded concern. A worst-case scenario is as follows:

Dr. Smith is treating Mrs. Finicky, and informally consults Dr. Jones about her care. Dr. Smith's case presentation begins as follows "This is a 45-year-old woman with a two month history of. . ." No name is given, and Dr. Jones never sees the patient. Following a discussion about possible diagnostic and treatment alternatives, Dr. Smith writes in the chart "Case discussed with Dr. Jones."

If Mrs. Finicky sues following an unfavorable outcome, it is likely that everyone whose name is noted in the medical record will be named in the lawsuit. When Dr. Jones is asked about the case, either in an initial investigation or during a deposition, the conversation with the lawyer will likely follow something along these lines:

Lawyer: "Dr. Jones, did you evaluate Mrs. Finicky as a consultant for Dr. Smith?"
Dr. Jones: "No, I did not."
Lawyer: "But Dr. Jones, your name is in the medical record."
Dr. Jones: "Yes, Dr. Smith and I may have discussed the case."
Lawyer: "Dr. Jones, are you saying you didn't personally examine Mrs. Finicky?"

Dr. Jones: "That is correct. I have never examined or evaluated Mrs. Finicky. Dr. Smith may have discussed her case with me. We frequently discuss our cases with each other."

Lawyer: "Why would you do that?"

Dr. Jones: "We discuss cases in order to get the opinion of another practitioner. We believe that this improves the quality of the patient care in our practices."

Juries love this kind of testimony. It goes a long way toward demonstrating that you value the opinions of others, and that you are not one of those physicians who is seen as arrogantly flapping around in *status narcissisticus.* *

*This wonderful visual image was coined by Dr. Thomas Gutheil and used during his presentations.

The only possible problem with the curbside consult is that if your colleague gives you bad advice, and you take it, you are liable, not your casually consulted colleague. Unless Dr. Smith formally requests a consultation and Dr. Jones evaluates Mrs. Finicky (or in some jurisdictions just her medical record), duty has not been established.

Caveat

Curbside consultations are not a replacement for a formal evaluation by a specialist. Curbside consults are usually requested by physicians who would not otherwise consider requesting a formal consult (or could not justify it in a capitated/ managed care setting). If you request a curbside consult (or get asked about one), make it clear that this is what is being sought. In order to have established duty, either the patient must be interviewed/examined or the chart reviewed (depending on state statutes). Liability for the requesting physician (consultee) is established as follows: if the consultee wholeheartedly implements the consultant's suggestions, and a similarly trained and experienced physician would not have, the consultee is responsible for what happens to the patient as a result of a curbside consultation. This is also true in formal consultations, but the liability would be shared because *both* physicians have the duty in formal consults.

Process Issues

Processes are all of the "things" that you, your staff, or your organization do which affect or involve the patient, not just the actual evaluation and treatment. Processes are generally system issues, and even the smallest practice should have some mechanism to identify the areas that are "high risk/high volume" for your specific area of practice. Some of these issues fall into either the Bad Feeling/Bad Outcome part of the liability equation. Suggestions for limiting your liability due to administrative processes are as follows:

- Have a system in place to ensure that all ordered tests (lab, X-ray, etc.) are reported, and that you have a clearly defined system for feedback and follow-up

- Conduct an annual brainstorming session with your staff to review the "soup to nuts" processes that affect your practice (e.g. ease of making appointments, directions to your office, parking, availability of childcare facilities, patient rights & responsibilities visibly posted, cleanliness of bathroom, correction of billing errors, etc.)

- Have a system in place where staff, patients, and visitors can provide you with feedback (anonymously if they choose) on anything that can be improved

When others know that you are interested in their ideas, it goes a long way to ensuring their trust. If at all possible, implement some of the suggestions you are given as soon as possible. Train your staff to be able to handle patient complaints and to know when to seek assistance from someone up the chain.

References

Beckman HB, Markakis KM, Suchman AL et al: **The Doctor-Patient Relationship and Malpractice: :Lessons From Plaintiff Depositions**. *Arch Intern Med* 154:1365-1370, 1994

Berner M: Write Smarter, Not Longer.
The Mental Health Practitioner and the Law.
Ed. Lifson LE and Simon RI.
Harvard Univ Press, Cambridge, 1998

Crane M: **Malpractice Survey**. *Medical Economics* 26 July 99

Documentation Guidelines for Evaluation and Management Services. *Medicare B Newsletter*, Nov 1994.

Levinson W, Roter DL, Mullooly JP et al: **Physician-Patient Communication: The Relationship With Malpractice Claims Arising From Primary Care Physicians and Surgeons**. *JAMA* 277:553-559, 1997

Marvel MK, Epstein RM, Flowers K et. al: **Soliciting the Patient's Agenda – Have We Improved?** *JAMA* 281:283-287, 1999

6. Special Issues in Managed Care

The advent of managed care in the United States has brought with it many changes in the way physicians practice, and in particular, a concern about a variety of potential conflicts of interest. Physicians are forced to balance the competing interests of providing quality patient care against that of income considerations. For the purposes of this discussion, the terms **managed care organizations (MCO)** and **health maintenance organizations (HMO)** will be used synonymously, although an HMO is just one kind of MCO.

Economic Informed Consent

Patients must be appraised of their diagnoses, the risks and benefits of the recommended treatment, the risks and benefits of the alternative treatments, and the prognosis if no treatment is provided. One of the issues pertinent to those who are healthcare providers in MCOs is to ensure that patients are informed about *all* alternative treatments, even if they are not covered in the plan. Economic informed consent means that clinicians have an ethical duty to inform patients about any and all aspects that could impact on their care.

Gag Clauses

Gag clauses are imposed by an MCO on physicians, and involve limiting the information given to patients, such as medications not on the formulary, treatments not covered, or financial benefits the organization may gain from limiting care, etc. Because they violate ethical and legal principles, most states now have statutes which make gag clauses illegal.

There is an obvious potential conflict of interest in any managed care system where a physician is not remunerated beyond a certain **base rate** (also called a **capitation rate**) for treating a patient with a certain condition. Costs incurred over the capitation rate are usually paid out of a risk pool. With larger MCOs there is more shared risk, although even then there is still the ever-present concern about the bottom line. An example of limiting treatment with a need for economic informed consent is as follows:

In the mid 1990's, many managed care formularies did not offer any of the **selective serotonergic reuptake inhibitors (SSRIs)** for treating depression. They offered only the older **tricyclic antidepressants (TCAs)**. TCAs have been available for a much longer time, and are effective in the treatment of depression. Unfortunately, many TCAs have significant side effects that range from unpleasant to life-threatening. SSRIs are now considered first-line medications in the treatment of depression, and most MCOs have altered their formulary policies.

In any situation like this, each specialty should lobby to have acceptable medications on formulary, or ensure that a process is in place to fill off-formulary prescriptions. *Clinicians cannot tell patients only about the alternatives authorized by the MCO – they must discuss all appropriate alternatives.* Patients can be told about alternative forms of treatment that are available at additional cost. *Avoid collusion with the MCO.*

Patients can voice their displeasure to the MCO about its coverage. If enough people in a plan complain, organizations will either become more flexible, or lose their market share. If the issue receives a lot of political press, changes may be legislated (such as making gag clauses unlawful).

SOC in Managed Care

Managed care has caused a marked shift from inpatient to outpatient treatment in every specialty. This has had an effect on the applicable SOC in clinical practice, but not in the courts. Although it is likely that the courts will eventually recognize this shift, the legal standard is unchanged for medical care given in a managed care environment. This is one of many dilemmas facing physicians practicing in MCOs. Where primary care physicians previously referred patients with certain diagnoses to specialists, they no longer have the authorization to do so. They may be required to care for patients suffering from conditions that they have limited experience in treating.

Limitation of Service and Referrals

Physicians are offered a variety of financial incentives if they can avoid making referrals and providing costly forms of treatment. Legal difficulties can often be avoided if you:

1. Disclose to the patient the presence of any conflicts of interest (e.g. financial incentives to limit treatment).

2. Do not exceed your level of expertise.

3. Choose the less expensive of two treatment choices as long as they have identical outcome data (or that have statistically insignificant variation).

In the early 1990's, a group of specialists made a transition from a fee-for-service practice to full managed care capitation over a three-month period. While their patient base remained the same, the number of **coronary artery bypass graft procedures (CABGs)** performed was halved in the year following the transition. The question from this situation is "Were there an inappropriately high number of CABGs being performed previously (perhaps based on higher remuneration), or are there a large number of CABGs that are now not being performed to keep costs down?"

Data such as in the above example have been collected from many specialty areas. It would be helpful if a clear and convincing answer could be found. In order to make data-driven decisions, all specialties are collecting outcome data on patients with certain diseases and in particular treatment groups. Physicians working for MCOs have ethical duties unique to this environment.

Duty to Disclose

Duty to disclose involves discussing the economic implications of treatment choices with patients. An important case regarding the duty to disclose financial incentives involved a woman who brought forth a lawsuit on behalf of her late husband (who died from an MI). He had been experiencing chest pain, but had not been referred to a cardiologist. The plaintiff argued that if the attending physician had disclosed the financial incentives to not make referrals to specialists, the couple would have paid to see a specialist on their own.

Duty to Appeal Adverse Decisions

In *Wickline v. California* in 1986, the California Court of Appeals found that managed care reviewers can be held liable for decisions which adversely affect patient care.

What *Wickline v. California* also established is that when there is an injury to a patient because of premature discharge from a hospital (following denial of benefits), the person responsible is not the managed care reviewer or the MCO. It is the discharging physician – particularly if the decision to deny further benefits was not appealed. If, in your medical judgment (not for secondary reasons such as the patient's convenience), the patient should not be discharged from the hospital, then do not do so. Instead, assist the patient in an aggressive appeal, and ask a physician colleague to assist you in this process.

Hospitalization, discharge, conducting specific tests or providing treatment are *clinical decisions*, and must be made in the best interests of the patient.

"In matters of style, swim with the current; in matters of principle, stand like a rock."

Thomas Jefferson

Getting support from the MCO to provide proper patient care will be getting at least somewhat easier over the next several years because of current, and upcoming, reforms.

ERISA

The **Employee Retirement Income Security Act (ERISA)** was passed in 1974. It was initially enacted after several scandalous cases of companies declaring bankruptcy, and the employees losing all of their retirement income and benefits. The aim of this act was to protect private employer retirement plans (and the retirement benefits of workers) from lawsuits. It applies to employer-purchased health plans.

The unintended effect of ERISA is that it has sheltered MCOs from lawsuits alleging medical negligence or bad faith benefits administration. Because ERISA is a federal statute, MCOs can claim that any state law allowing lawsuits can be pre-empted. If health benefits are purchased independently of employment, this argument becomes invalid, and the MCO can be sued.

To date, MCOs have successfully hidden behind the protection of ERISA and avoided all but minimal liability in medical malpractice cases. MCOs have generally been held legally accountable only for the cost of the denied treatments.

Some patients have passed away while waiting for their lawsuits to proceed through the appeals process. In one of the most extreme cases, a patient with cardiac problems (who was enrolled in an HMO) had to wait several months while appealing the denial for coverage of cardiac surgery. It was finally approved, but by that time, his condition had deteriorated to the point that he needed a heart transplant. This too was denied, and he died while appealing this decision. The first breakthrough of the ERISA wall came in 1995. The Third Circuit Court of Appeals held that an MCO could be sued for vicarious liability in cases of medical negligence.

In 1997, Texas and Missouri passed legislation allowing lawsuits for similar actions. Georgia and California followed with similar legislation in 1999. Twenty-nine states considered bills in 1998, and 32 in 1999. MCO liability is one of the prominent (and hotly disputed) items on the current Patient Protection Bill. The detractors argue that the cost of the additional lawsuits will markedly increase the costs of health plans (with the unspoken obvious effect of eating into employer profits). A 9% increase in costs was predicted. In Texas, only a 1% increase has been recorded (thus far). The advocates for such legislation argue that MCOs have vastly overestimated the number of potential lawsuits. There have been only five cases in the past two years which are being appealed in Texas courts.

Patient Protection Bills

During the late 1990's, several patient protection bills went before Congress, and were the subject of significant partisan debate.

Three major issues are common to the patient protection bills which have been introduced over the past several years:

- The patient's ability to sue the MCO for refusal to provide care

- Direct access to specialists without having to go through the primary care "gatekeeper"

- Doctors should make patient-care decisions, and define what constitutes "medical necessity" (instead of managed care administrators doing so)

In October 1999, many observers were surprised when a non-partisan bill (HR 2723) known as the Norwood-Dingell Patient's Bill of Rights, was passed by the House of Representatives in a startling 275-151 victory (highlighting how important these issues have become with constituents over the past several years). The prominent issues of the bill include:

- "Medical necessity" decisions will be made by physicians (currently, the MCO determines what is considered medically necessary)

- An independent appeals process will be guaranteed (addressing the "fox-guarding-the-hen-house" concerns)

- Patients will have direct access to obstetricians and pediatricians (which is a big improvement over previous referral procedures for these specialties)

- The "prudent layperson" standard for emergency care will be applied (meaning that if a "reasonable" person would think the condition is more likely than not an emergency, it will be covered as an emergency. This will eliminate nonpayment if the discharge diagnosis is not typically one considered to be an emergency)

- Gag clauses will be eliminated

- Patients will have the right to sue in state court if a care plan denies a medically necessary treatment (eliminating the ERISA-based preemption)

At the time of writing, the next step in this process is a bill that will be addressed in conference in the Senate, with final legislation expected to pass in 2000.

Health Maintenance Organization (HMO) Liability

As discussed above, where courts have held that HMO liability was limited by ERISA, damages have been limited only to the cost of treatments which were not authorized. However, the most recent trend in rulings seems to be moving toward expanding MCOs' responsibility for the consequences of denial of care.

An interesting twist is the voiced intent by several law firms (some being involved in the very successful lawsuits against the tobacco companies) to bring actions against several of the large MCOs. The desire to sue MCOs is of course not new, but the basis of these proposed lawsuits is not medical malpractice cases that hold MCOs responsible for denial of care, but something entirely new.

Legal firms are bringing suit under some older federal regulations, one of which is known as the **Racketeering**

Influence and Corrupt Organization Act (RICO). The plan is to charge HMOs on the grounds that they use fear tactics and threats of decreased income to force physicians to limit care. One federal judge has dismissed a lawsuit filed on this basis (it is very difficult to prove), but others will follow.

While it is as yet undetermined that such lawsuits will be successful, Wall Street has taken heed, with several stock prices declining after the intent to sue was made public.

There are assaults on MCOs from many areas. Managed healthcare will be one of the most hotly debated issues in politics in the early years of the new millennium.

The most helpful outcome would incorporate the benefits of managed care (the ethical cost containment measures that can ensure or improve the quality of care), while minimizing the negative consequences that come from putting financial incentives above the best interests of the patient.

Scope of Care and Referrals

An additional concern voiced by many physicians is the pressure to limit specialist referrals. Theoretically, doctors have the right to delete procedures from their scope of practice (defined by the healthcare plan). However, given the overt and covert pressures involved in medical practice, this may not be easily accomplished.

An example of a "gray zone" scope-of-practice concern would be a family practice physician whose practice includes treadmill stress tests or the evaluation of GI bleeding with sigmoidoscopy. With adequate training and experience, there is no concern with any physician performing these procedures. The question of IC arises – how much should a patient be told if a physician performs a somewhat risky procedure on an occasional basis?

What is important is that physicians practice within their expertise and comfort level for procedures and services. The "plan" is not responsible if you exceed your level of competence and fall beneath the SOC – you are.

Physician-Reviewers

Inroads have been made regarding the accountability of physicians who review treatment requests for MCOs. In several states, these reviews are now considered to be an aspect of medical practice. The implications are that the physician-reviewer can be held accountable for charges of medical negligence, even if they can't be sued under the ERISA preemption. A new wrinkle involves the issue of whether a physician in one state can make a treatment decision (e.g. denying treatment) concerning a patient in another state without being charged with "practicing medicine without a license."

Who Makes Treatment Decisions?

For the past several years, one of the issues causing considerable outcry among patients and physicians has been over who makes treatment decisions. Although the MCO would make the decision of approval or denial, the physician was held accountable if she followed this decision and there was an unfavorable outcome. Even if an appeal was made to the MCO and denied, physicians were still held responsible.

A somewhat startling, yet welcome change occurred in late 1999 when the UnitedHealth Group announced they would no longer require a reviewer to approve physicians' treatment decisions prior to treatment (called pretreatment authorization). Exceptions to this policy change include decisions for mental health care, and the requirement to review some prescriptions. Although considered a huge advance for patients and physicians, this was also a sound business decision. After an extensive study, UnitedHealth discovered that they spent over $100 million to pay for the pretreatment authorization process and denied requests less than 1% of the time. In the future they will review their data and decide whether this change was a cost-effective one.

Several states (including Maryland, Virginia, and North Carolina) are taking medication decisions away from the MCO care plans, and having physicians make them instead. Physicians are being told they can use non-formulary medications (to varying degrees) if they believe that a non-formulary agent is medically indicated.

Other Ethical Issues

Conflicts of Interest

It cannot be overemphasized that physicians must put the interest of patients ahead of any potential self-interest.

More formal guidelines are forthcoming. The Supreme Court has agreed to hear a case in which it is alleged that an incentive bonus structure in a physician-owned HMO caused financial gain to become more of a priority than patient care. The physician, health plan, and insurance company all appealed the decision of the Illinois Court, which found the physician responsible for delay of care. The decision of the Supreme Court has a far-reaching impact on the financial incentives MCOs use for physicians.

Another issue causing concern is whether it is acceptable to lie in order to obtain coverage for patients. In a recent survey, 39% of physicians reported that they lied at least once to help patients obtain coverage for services. Many exaggerated the severity of their patients' conditions to avoid early hospital discharge. Others said they reported symptoms the patient did not have in order to secure coverage. Another group stated they changed the billing diagnoses to help patients secure coverage.

Another 37% of physicians reported that their patients had asked them to deceive a third-party payer. Forty-eight percent of physicians recommended that patients pay for uncovered services out of their own pockets.

An extreme case which highlights the risks involved in misrepresentation is as follows. A physician wanted to order a CT of the head for his patient with liver cancer in order to rule out cerebral metastases. In order to get coverage, the doctor wrote "brain tumor" as the principal diagnosis. The patient received the bill with this diagnosis printed on it. She then hung herself. Lying about coding (or anything on the medical record) places you at risk for fraud also.

Caveat
The recommendation made both by lawyers and ethicists, is that physicians should act as the patient's advocate.

This issue of advocacy has been a frequent topic of discussion amongst psychiatrists who do inpatient work. Their concern is over the very strict (and many think inappropriate) criteria that patients must meet in order to gain admission (and to avoid premature discharge). Frequently, reports are made which overestimate the severity of a patient's risk for harm to self or others, just to secure the minimum treatment that the treating psychiatrist deems necessary.

The problem arises when the psychiatrist continues to exaggerate the patient's suicidal or homicidal risk after admission. Documentation about diminished risk may only be present on the day of discharge. Regardless of whether or not the patient was at the level of risk detailed in the MCO report, the "retrospectoscope" may be very unkind. Cross-examination of the inpatient psychiatrist could go something like this:

Lawyer: "Now, Dr. Froyd, although you discharged Ms. Smith on day 7 of her hospitalization, your note in the record from the day before states that she remained a high risk for self harm. Is that correct?"

Dr. Froyd: "Um, er, well you see, um. . ."

Lawyer: "What did you say doctor? I couldn't hear you."

You are then stuck with either telling the jury that you lied to ensure she could stay in the hospital (and expound on the woes of managed care, which doesn't go over well at all), or you need to come up with what miraculous thing changed in a 12 hour period that now makes the patient safe for discharge (and that you apparently didn't document).

It is much better to discuss your concerns with the patient and the family at the time of admission. You can then help them appeal any MCO decision that you feel is medically inappropriate (such as early discharge). As noted, it is now increasingly common for the MCOs to have physician-reviewers for particular specialties. These physicians are increasingly aware that there have been licensure actions for medical negligence, and that formal liability actions may occur in the near future.

Of course, the appeals process may span from days to weeks. At times you may have to admit or keep the patient in the hospital with no guarantee of payment.

Caveat

Denial of treatment by an MCO means only that payment for treatment has been declined, not that treatment isn't required. Only you can make the actual treatment decisions, putting you in a double bind as the treating physician.

References

Bozeman FC: **Are the Skies Clearing in Managed Care? Maybe, But Keep Umbrellas Handy**.
Escambia County Med Society Bulletin 29(10):5, 1999

Council on Ethical and Judicial Affairs: **Ethical Issues in Managed Care**.
JAMA 273:330-335, 1995

Dukes v. United States Healthcare, Inc., 57 F.3d 350 (3rd Cir. 1995)

Foubister V: **Is it OK to Lie to Your Patients**?
AMA News 42:1, 30, 1999

Freeman VG, Rathore SS, Weinfurt KP et al: **Lying for Patients: Physician Deception of Third-Party Payers**.
Arch Intern Med 159:2263-2270, 1999

Kaplan A: **Medical Necessity: What Is It?**
Psychiatric Times 16(12):38-40, 1999

King JV, Liang BA: **The Silencing of the Physician: Gag Rules in a Managed Care Environment**.
Hospital Physician, 1998

Klein SA: **Hard-Hitting Lawyers Launch New Assault on Managed Care**.
AMA News 42(39):1, 29-30, 1999

Kuhl v. Lincoln National Health Plan of Kansas City, Inc.
999 F.2nd 298 (8th Cir 1993)

Miller TE, Sage WM: **Disclosing Physician Financial Incentives**.
JAMA 281:1424-1430, 1999

Newcomer LN: **Who Should Determine When Health Care is Medically Necessary?**
NEJM 341:58-59, 1999

Page L: **Texas Law on HMO Liability Generates Little Cost – So Far**.
AMA News 42:11,13, 1999

Rice B: **The Newest Threat: Pressure to go Beyond Your Expertise**.
Medical Economics 76:119-120

Shea v. Esenstein,
107 F.3d 625(8th Cir. 1997), cert. denied 118 S. Ct. 297(1997)

States Agree MDs Should Make Drug Decisions.
Psychiatric Times 34:5, 1999

Welch B: **Managed Care Litigation: The Foundation is Laid.**
Psychiatric Times Aug:11-14, 1999

Wickline v. State, CA. App. (1986)

Wilson v. Blue Cross, CA. App (1990)

Wing K: ***The Law and the Public's Health***.
Health Administration Press, Chicago, 1999

7. Regulatory Stuff

While the information in this chapter may at times seem outrageous, remember regulatory controls are one method of controlling healthcare costs while attempting to increase quality. Unfortunately, many innocent (or at least mildly oblivious) clinicians have been caught in the webs spun by regulatory agencies.

Physicians are more likely to encounter liability difficulties from regulatory agencies than from any other source. The regulatory arena is ground that has become increasingly fertile and well-tilled in the past few years. The full harvest has yet to come. The contents of this chapter are as follows:

- **Healthcare Fraud and Abuse Regulations:** False Claims Act, Medicare/Medicaid Fraud and Abuse Law

- **State Agencies:** Particularly boards of licensure, which oversee many issues that are considered to be professional negligence

- **Conflict of Interest Regulations:** Ethical Referrals and Antikickback Statutes

- **Other Regulations:** such as EMTALA and ADA

- **Other Regulatory Agencies:** OSHA and EEOC

- **Regulatory Advisories:** Federal Register

Federal Regulatory Agencies

There are many federal regulatory agencies involved in the practice of medicine. This may not surprise you. What may be surprising, however, is that these agencies may have a far greater potential to seriously damage your practice and earning potential than a garden-variety medical malpractice suit.

The Department of Health and Human Services (DHHS)

This is the principal agency involved in protecting the health care of all Americans, and providing essential human services. Some of the agencies which fall under the DHHS, are (in acronymical splendor): CDC, FDA, NIH, IHS, and HCFA.

The Health Care Finance Administration (HCFA)

The HFCA administers the Medicare, Medicaid, and Children's Health Insurance Programs. It is one of the largest regulatory agencies.

The **Office of the Inspector General (OIG)** investigates allegations of abuse. Felony violations are prosecuted by the **Department of Justice (DOJ)**. Consider the following factoids:

- In 1999, the DOJ declared that healthcare fraud is its number two priority for the new millennium (right behind violent crime)

- The federal government has committed $4.5 billion dollars over the next six years toward enforcing various anti-fraud statutes

The anti-fraud statutes apply to anyone who receives funds from a federal agency (most notably from Medicare and Medicaid).

One of the most interesting of the federal anti-fraud laws is the **False Claims Act**. The original statute was passed during the Civil War to curtail the many suppliers who were charging the Union Army and federal government outrageous prices for supplies (this was the 1860's version of the $700 ashtray). The Act stated that it was illegal for anyone to knowingly charge the government more than an item was worth. The resurgence in popularity of this law occurred when it was updated in 1986 to have more "teeth" for enforcement. The federal government began to hold contractors responsible on many fronts for their overcharging practices. The term "whistleblower" entered our lexicon as someone who reported fraudulent activities to the government. With the exponential increase in demand for medical care, the number of fraudulent claims being submitted under Medicare also increased. The application of the False Claims Act to healthcare spending became a new and powerful focus. How does this apply to physicians?

Few would argue that the small number of physicians who defraud the government *should* be held accountable for their actions. How does this pertain to the average physician?

Caveat

There is no requirement on the government's part to prove that you *intentionally* committed fraud. Even if you unknowingly submit a false claim (and should have been aware of this), you can be fined. You can also be penalized for unfulfilled supervisory responsibilities. Further, the penalty can be a loss of your Medicare eligibility. Professional liability insurance will not cover your losses (or your legal costs).

Formula for Arriving at the Amount of the Fine for Fraud Cases

$5,000 to $10,000 per false claim
+
Three times the amount of the claim

If this isn't scary enough, there is another element. . .

Along Comes HIPAA

Health care fraud is estimated to amount to between $80 and $100 billion dollars per year. This is one-tenth of all healthcare spending! The Kennedy-Kasselbaum Bill was passed in 1996 and is formally known as the **Health Insurance Portability and Accountability Act (HIPAA) of 1996**. HIPAA put new teeth into the False Claims Act by creating new healthcare fraud crimes, such as making false statements and embezzlement involving public or private healthcare plans or contracts.

HIPAA extended the ability of many Americans to maintain their healthcare insurance after termination of employment, and to decrease the exclusions for pre-existing conditions. It is only upon reading the act it in its entirety that the far-reaching consequences become obvious. The initial focus of the expanded fraud and abuse crackdown was aimed at laboratories. Settlements in these cases reclaimed *hundreds of millions of dollars*.

The next investigation involved over 5,000 hospitals, and involved scrutiny of "unbundling" lab charges. This refers to the practice of billing tests on an individual basis instead of on standardized groupings. For example, an SMA-6 would be billed as six tests instead of clustering Na, K, Cl, CO_2, glucose, & BUN together. Another investigation identified tens of thousands of patient transfers that were improperly billed to Medicare as discharges (transfers are remunerated at a lesser amount).

Another area of focus was the investigation of teaching hospitals for billing Medicare for services provided by physicians in supervisory roles. Several large, well-known universities were fined up to $30 million dollars. The plan over the next several years is to audit every teaching program, which is called the **Physicians in Academic Teaching Hospitals (PATH)** audit.

The arms of HIPPA seem to be everywhere. Just when you thought you could take a sigh of relief, two seemingly innocuous words leap out at you – qui tam.

Qui Tam

A *qui tam* action occurs when an individual is granted authority (by statute) to bring a lawsuit against any individual or organization on behalf of the government. If the lawsuit is successful, individuals are given a percentage of the "spoils." The infamous investigations of the 1980's in defense contracting were *qui tam* actions. Because of the numerous cases brought by employees ("whistleblowers"), other laws had to be passed. These were the so-called Whistleblower Protection Acts, which prohibit retaliation after a complaint has been filed.

Qui tam actions allow anyone to bring an action against you under the False Claims Act. A colleague, an employee, a patient, or anyone who has an axe to grind can launch a *qui tam* action.

These actions are first reported to the DOJ, which investigates about 20% of all allegations. If the defendant is fined, the person bringing the action (known as the **responder**) gets 15 to 20% of the amount collected. If the DOJ does not pursue the action, the responder can bring a lawsuit to court. If the responder wins the civil suit, she can receive up to 30% of the amount. *Qui tam* actions are increasing each year, as lawyers and others become aware of the possibilities. A search of *qui tam* on the internet will return thousands of hits with hundreds of law firms. . . just waiting for someone to call.

Consider the following knee-weakening scenario:

You have a part-time employee doing your billing. The CBCs and LFTs you have ordered over the past six months have been "unbundled" into their components (i.e. CBCs were billed as H/H, WBC, platelet count, MCV, MCH and MCHC; LFTs were billed as SGOT, SGPT, LDH and ALK PHOS). The difference between the CBC cost and the unbundled charges can be $50 (or more). For each unbundled claim, you can be fined up to $10,150. If this happened 20 times, you could be hit with a fine of $203,000 – for which you alone are responsible.

In addition to fines (and occasional prison sentences), you may also lose your medical license, staff privileges, and your ability to participate in any federal health care programs, particularly Medicare, Medicaid, and the **Civilian Health and Medical Program of the Uniformed Services (CHAMPUS)**. This process is called being "formally sanctioned and excluded."

Caveat
The OIG of the DHHS has wide discretionary powers to exclude physicians for a number of offenses. In addition to being found guilty of violating one of the regulations or laws noted in this chapter, you can also be excluded for:

- Being convicted of a "controlled substances" offense

- Loss of professional license

- Submission of bills substantially in excess of usual charges

- Defaulting on student loans

The exclusion is usually for a fixed period (usually 5 years), and frequently results in disciplinary action by the state licensing boards, as well as a report being sent to the NPDB.

Anti-Conflict of Interest Laws
Two laws regulating conflict of interest at the federal level are the **Antikickback Statute** and the **Ethics in Patients Referral Act**. Many states have similar statutes.

Antikickback Statute
This is part of the anti-fraud and abuse provision in Medicare and Medicaid programs. This statute prohibits anyone from receiving monetary benefit (or any other type of benefit) from the act of referring patients when Medicare or Medicaid is paying

for any service or item (or any part thereof). This is a felony punishable by up to five years imprisonment, or a fine of $25,000, or both.

Ethics in Patient Referral Act

This is also known as the **Stark Laws (or Stark I and II Laws)**, named for Rep. "Pete" Stark. This act prohibits Medicare and Medicaid from paying for any service that physicians provide or order through an entity in which they have a financial interest. The goal of this act is to prohibit self-referral fees. Stark I was passed in 1989 and dealt primarily with laboratories. Stark II, passed in 1995, deals with everything else.

It can become confusing as to what exactly is allowed under these various laws. The HCFA developed and published several exceptions (called **safe harbors**) to these laws. As of the date of writing there are 23. Dealing with these laws has become a legal subspecialty all its own, and another situation in which you don't want to rely solely on the advice of Cousin Joe.

Given the massive confusion and murkiness over what is legal, HIPAA and the Balanced Budget Act of 1997 authorized individuals to request advisory opinions from the OIG. The OIG will provide an opinion about whether an action will be in violation of the Antikickback or Stark Laws. The catch is that those requesting assistance may well be investigated (and prosecuted). You have the option to withdraw your request before an opinion is formally issued. Also of assistance is the DHHS website – www.dhhs.gov – no fuss, no frills, no risk.

Caveat
If you have to ask whether or not something is OK, it probably isn't.

State Regulatory Agencies
Most states have their own variations of federal law, or have the authority to act on behalf of the federal government.

The one agency about which you will be most familiar is your state licensing board, usually called something like the Department of Professional Regulation. They can provide much of the state-specific information discussed in this book.

Most states also have their own prohibited referral and remuneration laws. These restrictions are available, along with all other regulatory information, from your state board of medicine. A significant percentage of the published disciplinary actions against physicians are the result of violations of self-referral laws. Anyone can make a formal complaint about you to your state board of licensure. These complaints (often called **allegations of professional misconduct**), may result from:

- A specific case (e.g. an alleged act of medical negligence for which the plaintiff was unable to interest a lawyer in taking the case)

- A pattern of poor care

- A concern about an impaired physician or moral unfitness (usually a complaint related to a sexual relationship with a patient)

- Patient abandonment

- Performing unauthorized services

Once a complaint is filed with a state board, the allegations are usually heard before a committee. If the complaint seems unfounded or frivolous, it may be dropped. If, following investigation, the complaint is found to have validity, the committee follows specific procedures for each stage of the investigation (and physicians are provided full due process). The penalties can involve:

- License revocation
- License suspension
- Reprimand
- Censure

Ensure that your legal counsel gets involved early in the administrative process (ideally at the time you are notified of a complaint). A claim of negligence to a Board of Medicine can also be used against you in a subsequent medical malpractice claim on the same issue.

Caveat
Administrative actions can be more damaging (and expensive) than medical malpractice cases.

Other Regulatory Stuff
While there are many statutes and regulations that affect physicians, one that is essential for you to be aware of is EMTALA.

EMTALA is the **Emergency Medical Treatment and Active Labor Act of 1986**. It is also known as the **Anti-Dumping Law**. It states that all hospitals receiving Medicare funding must provide medical screening for anyone who comes to the ER.

EMTALA is enforced by the HCFA. Violations of EMTALA can result in civil actions brought forth by individuals or the HCFA. The HCFA can impose fines up to $50,000 per violation (against the facility and/or the doctor), and can terminate the Medicare provider status of the hospital or physician. A civil action under EMTALA does not preclude a patient from filing a malpractice claim – in fact, most EMTALA lawsuits are coupled with medical negligence claims.

EMTALA was enacted following several nasty cases when patients, who were unable to pay for medical assistance, were turned away from ERs without care. They either died or suffered serious injuries as a result of not receiving treatment.

Under EMTALA, after the required medical screening exam, if a patient is considered to have an emergency, certain steps must be taken. An **emergency medical condition** is defined as: *a medical condition manifesting itself by acute symptoms of sufficient severity including severe pain, psychiatric disturbances and/or symptoms of substance abuse such that the absence of immediate medical attention could reasonably be expected to result in: a) placing the health of the individual in serious jeopardy, b) serious impairment to bodily functions, or c) serious dysfunction to any bodily organ or part, or with respect to a pregnant woman who is having contractions (i) there is an inadequate time to effect a safe transfer to another hospital for delivery or (ii) that transfer may pose a threat to the health or safety of the woman or the unborn child."*

All patients who do have an emergency medical condition must then be stabilized within the capacity of the institution, regardless of the ability to pay. The definition of **stabilization** from the statute is as follows: *Stabilization means, with respect to an emergency medical condition, that no material deterioration of the condition is likely, within reasonable medical probability, to result from or occur, during the transfer of the patient from a facility (or discharge).* This law also requires that specialists attend the patient as needed to assist with stabilization.

To transfer a patient to another hospital the following conditions must be met:

- The patient must be stabilized (to the ability of the hospital)

- The patient must request and consent to the transfer

- If the patient is unable to consent, it must be in the best interests of the patient (the receiving hospital is better able to care for the condition), not because the hospital is inconvenienced by a non-paying patient

- The receiving physician must accept and agree to treat the patient

- The receiving hospital must agree to accept the patient and provide treatment

- The mode of transportation must be appropriate for the level of care necessary

- Copies of the medical record must accompany the patient

Caveat
Any hospital or organization with an emergency room must be knowledgeable about the specifications of EMTALA.

A recent Supreme Court case ruled that the plaintiff does not need to show that there was an improper motive on the part of the defendant healthcare facility or physician, only that the care provided was different from that which would be given in a similar situation.

It is important to differentiate between a violation of EMTALA and medical negligence. A defendant can meet the obligations under EMTALA, but have failed to meet the SOC for a specific evaluation or treatment. This is a quality of care issue, and should be addressed through the medical negligence process, not as a violation of EMTALA.

One sticky area is the conflict between the requirement of many managed care plans for preauthorization of emergency care and the EMTALA requirements. Many states have statutes banning the preauthorization requirement for emergency care, and this probably will be addressed in the Federal Patient Rights Bill (expected in 2000). Larger facilities with ERs are aware of this conflict, and have developed ways of addressing it.

ADA

The 1990 **Americans with Disabilities Act (ADA)** guarantees certain rights for disabled individuals, and applies to organizations with 15 or more employees.

Definition

The ADA defines someone as "disabled" when he or she:

- has a physical or mental disorder that substantially limits one or more significant life activities,

- has a history of such a disorder,

- or can be perceived as having such a disorder.

There are four **titles** of the ADA: employment, public services and transportation, public accommodations, and telecommunications. The **Equal Employment Opportunity Commission (EEOC)** has the responsibility of enforcing the ADA.

The ADA protects qualified individuals with disabilities who, with or without reasonable accommodation, can perform the essential functions of the employment position.

Importance to Patients
The ADA plays a large role in protecting the rights of patients in many situations: insurance, ensuring actual physical access to healthcare facilities, protection from losing their livelihood based on a disability, eligibility for programs, etc.

Importance to Physicians
In addition to providing protection for patients, the ADA protects physicians from negative decisions made by healthcare organizations, credentialing bodies, state medical boards, and other organizations if decisions are based on the presence of physical or mental disorders (not simply impaired judgment).

Several cases that have gone to court because of (inappropriate) denial of privileges/licensure were because physicians had psychiatric diagnoses (with no evidence of impairment).

Bragdon v. Abbott
This 1998 Supreme Court case addressed the trend (being established by lower courts) that the ADA was providing less protection than intended. In 1994, a patient disclosed her HIV infection to her dentist during a visit to his private office in Bangor, Maine. She needed a cavity filled. Rather than performing this procedure at his office (as was customary), the dentist told her he would fill it only in a hospital setting, and that she would be responsible for the additional fees.

Ms. Abbott sued under Title III of the Act, which states that: *No individual shall be discriminated against on the basis of disability in the full and equal enjoyment of the goods, services, facilities, privileges, advantages, or accommodations of any place of public accommodation.* Public accommodation includes *a professional office of a healthcare provider.*

Before someone can receive protection under the law, she must meet the definition of disabled under the ADA. The Supreme Court had to decide whether an asymptomatic HIV infection was a *physical impairment* (point #1) that causes a *substantial limitation* (point #2) of one or more *major life activities* (point #3). The arguments in the lower courts were over whether an asymptomatic HIV infection substantially limits a major life activity. The Supreme Court, with three justices in dissent, found that HIV significantly limits sexual intercourse and reproduction. The court, not wishing their decision to be solely based on the limitation of reproduction, considered HIV seropositivity to have a profound impact on almost every phase of a person's life.

The result of this case is important to many HIV patients who wouldn't previously have been considered disabled if they were able to work, or their illness was controlled by medication.

Every state has antidiscrimination laws for people with disabilities. States may enact laws that are at least as protective of individual rights as is federal legislation. Some states also have HIV-specific statutes. The article by Gostin (1999) in the references provides an excellent state-by-state chart. The state laws often provide protection for those individuals who work for organizations with less than 15 employees. Anyone in business (including healthcare) needs to have a clear understanding of the legal obligation to provide the services specified in the ADA.

Interpreters & Translators
Much can be learned from a 1998 lawsuit against a hospital initiated by a hearing-impaired patient who was not offered a translator skilled in **American Sign Language (ASL)**. She was hospitalized against her will, but provided with neither medication nor treatment. She won the case. A large number of organizations and offices are unaware of their legal obligation to provide communication aids and assisted listening devices. The web address – www.nad.org – provides information on this and other requirements.

Other Regulatory Agencies & Acts

Two different acts/agencies that you should be aware of are:

Occupational, Safety, and Health Administration (OSHA)

OSHA is an administrative agency under the Department of Labor. It regulates private sector workplace safety and health matters. Its goal is to maximize the safety of workplaces, and minimize injuries to workers. The bible for OSHA issues is the **Occupational Safety and Health Administration Compliance Assistance Authorization Act of 1998.** OSHA's operating principle is that every employee has the right to a safe and healthful workplace.

The majority of large healthcare facilities are aware of OSHA regulations, but smaller practices may not be. Even if you are in solo practice and have only one employee, the rules still apply. At the small practice level, common sense prevails: no holes in walkways, no wires strung across the room, no obvious safety issues. Physicians may encounter problems if, when a formal complaint is registered, numerous prior complaints were found to have been made on a local level (and not dealt with).

Equal Employment Opportunity Commission (EEOC)

Many physicians would be surprised at how many complaints and lawsuits are lodged annually under Title VII of the Civil Rights Act. This is probably the most important federal antidiscrimination law, and it applies to all employers with 15 or more employees.

The EEOC prohibits employment discrimination based on race, color, religion, sex, and national origin (age is covered in a related act). Sexual harassment is also covered under this law. Since the mid-1990's, this area of civil litigation has become what one might term a "growth industry." Things in the workplace have changed because of Title VII. What used to be termed *harmless sexual banter* is no longer overlooked or discounted

("Boys will be boys"). There have been several actions against physicians who "just didn't get it" and continued to act inappropriately with female staff members. Also, if a patient behaves inappropriately and offends a staff member, you can't just ignore the issue. If the patient does not stop the offending comments/behavior after being politely asked to do so, it is highly advisable that you take further action (covered in Chapter 4). Adverse privileging and licensing actions have been undertaken for "unprofessional behavior." Organizations are no longer likely to tolerate the inappropriate behavior of the staff members. Now, the hospital board/MCO may become the target (through vicarious liability). As in other employment cases, if the employer knew or should have known of the offensive behavior, and did nothing about it, the case becomes difficult to defend. Physicians have also taken organizations to court under Title VII for alleged discrimination and harassment.

A good place to check for updates about regulatory matters is the *Federal Register*. Published weekly, the *Federal Register* contains regulations that are from the DHHS. The occasional perusal will ensure that you are not caught off guard on the variety of items that are passed into law. For example, the Federal Register, on 7/2/99, published HCFA 42 CFR Part 482 – "Medicare and Medicaid Programs: Hospital Conditions of Participation: Patients Rights." This long publication promulgated guidance for the following requirements:

- Notification to the patient of his rights

- Exercise of his rights in regard to his care

- Privacy and safety

- Confidentiality

- Freedom from the use of seclusion or restraint in any form unless clinically necessary

Physicians who are unaware of these regulations are still held liable, resulting in lawsuits and possible exclusion from being able to participate in government programs.

Monitoring current state and federal laws and regulations is within the domain of RM programs. While many requirements may not apply to small practices, physicians working in such settings still need to be informed of legal changes. If your practice has even a rudimentary regulatory compliance program, you are much more likely to have any improprieties deemed "honest mistakes" if you are audited or a complaint is initiated.

Professional Liability Insurance

Take a look at your professional liability insurance policy. Are you covered for the costs of legal defense in an administrative hearing before your state licensing board? What about your local privileging authority? Defending claims of fraud from a regulatory agency?

Some policies provide limited coverage for these instances. For claims filed against you for violations of regulatory codes, you may be able to get something called a "billing errors and compliance" policy or clause. Even if you have made an honest mistake, you may still have to pay for your defense (and be responsible for the penalties). Most insurance policies do not cover actions that involve dishonesty or fraud (just as medical malpractice insurance doesn't cover intentional torts).

Discuss the coverage that you do have with an attorney knowledgeable in this new and growing area of concern for physicians.

Caveat
"Laws too gentle are seldom obeyed; too severe, seldom executed."

Benjamin Franklin

References

Americans with Disabilities Act.
42 U.S. Code, sections 12101-12111

Beluck P: **In Crackdown On Health Care Fraud, U.S. Focuses On Training Hospitals and Clinics**.
New York Times. Dec 22, 1995:32

Bragdon v. Abbott, 118 S Ct 2196 (1998)

Bryan v. United States, 118 S Ct 1939, 1946-1947 (1998)

Davis JP: **Fraud and Abuse. Understanding the Stark II Proposed Regulations**.
Health Finance Man 52:65-69, 1998

DHHS Health Care Financing Administration 42 CFR Part 482
Medicare and Medicaid Programs: Hospital Conditions of Participation: Patient Rights.
Federal Register 64(127) 7/2/99

Ethics in Patient Referral Act, 42, USC Statute 1395nn (1998)

False Claims Act, 31 USC Statute 3729 (1997)

Federal Antikickback Statute, 42 USC Statute 1320a-7b (1998)

Foubister V: **Oregon Doctor Cited for Negligence for Undertreating Pain**.
Am Med News 42(36) p9, 1999

Fraud Charges Prompt New Coverage.
Psychiatric News Sept 17/21, 1999

Furrow BR, Johnson SH, Jost TS et al:
Health Law - Cases, Materials, and Problems, 2nd Edition.
West Publishing Company, St. Paul, 1991

Gostin LO, Feldblum C, Webber DW: **Disability Discrimination in America – HIV/AIDS and Other Health Conditions**.
JAMA 281(8): 745-52, 1999

Halevy A, Brody B: **Acquired Immunodeficiency Syndrome and the ADA: A Legal Duty to Treat**.
Am J Med 96:282-287, 1994

Hanlester Network v. Shalala, 51 F3d 1390, 1400 (9th Cir 1995)

Health Insurance Portability and Accountability Act of 1996.
Public Law, 104-191

Kalb PE: **Health Care Fraud and Abuse**.
JAMA 282:1163-1168, 1999

Klein S: **Supreme Court to Weigh Physician Financial Incentives**.
AMA News 42:1,7, 1999

Lipscomb J, Rosenstock L: **Healthcare Workers: Protecting Those Who Protect Our Health**.
Infection Control and Hospital Epidemiology 18(6), 1997

Psychiatrists Should Be Prepared to Treat Deaf Patients.
Psychiatric News 314:16,33, 1999

Public Law 105-241, 1998: Occupational Safety and Health Administration Compliance Assistance Authorization Act of 1998.

Sage WM: **Fraud and Abuse Law**.
JAMA 282:1179-1181, 1999

Schorr B: **Regardless of Payer Mix, No Dumping Permitted**.
Florida Medical Business 12(25):5, 1999

Serbarolli FJ: **Expanding the War on Health Care Fraud**.
The New York Law J March 18, 1997

Sokolow DS: **Congress Amends Law: New Advisory Opinions on Fraud and Abuse and Self-Referral Issues**.
FROF Articles. www.frof.com/articles, accessed 12/2/99

Wing KR: *The Law and the Public's Health*.
Health Administration Press, Chicago, 1999

Woody RH: *Legally Safe Mental Health Practice – Psycholegal Questions And Answers*.
Psychosocial Press, Madison CT, 1997

8. Organizational Stuff

Physicians face a myriad of organizational matters. Unfortunately, doctors are not aware of them unless given **on the job training (OJT)**, or find out about them the hard way. The topics in this chapter are:

- **Supervisory Relationships**
- **Credentialing & Privileging**
- **Contracts**
- **Other Liabilities**

Supervisory Relationships

This topic was introduced in Chapter 2 in the Vicarious Liability Section. Physicians are responsible for the medical care provided by many other professionals and staff members.

In many instances, physicians are unaware of this responsibility until they are in the midst of a lawsuit claiming negligent care (that was usually provided by someone for whom they were unaware they were liable).

The type of supervisory relationships that affect physicians (as supervisor or supervisee) are varied, but usually fall into one of the following categories:

- Formal – this involves a written contract or policy; this arrangement may involve formal supervision of a non-physician provider, or a physician without full privileges; you may be the designated preceptor for someone with privileges under a plan of supervision

- Informal – if you are the assigned staff member on a ward at a teaching hospital; this involves supervision of residents and medical students

For legal purposes, it is crucial to ensure that all parties clearly understand their respective roles and responsibilities. Your responsibilities should be made available in written form – either in the form of a policy or an SOP manual. If you are formally assigned to supervise an individual, a letter of appointment detailing each parties' responsibilities should be signed, as well as the duration of the supervisory relationship.

If you agree to supervise someone, you may be liable in one of two ways: first, for the negligent acts of anyone under your supervision (**respondeat superior**), and second, for negligent supervision.

An example of each of the occurrences is provided in the following example. An internal medicine resident starts a rotation on the CCU the first month after completing his PGY-1 year (internship). A newly admitted patient has congestive heart failure, and while currently stable, is in need of a Swan Ganz catheter. The new resident has seen several inserted and even assisted with one during internship, but has not done this unsupervised. He asks the clinical fellow on call for help, but she is out of the hospital. After discussing the case, she tells the resident to insert the catheter himself and to call her again if he encounters any difficulties. Dr. Murphy (of Murphy's Law) being alive and well (and seemingly spending countless hours inside hospitals) ensures that the catheter tip shears off and embolizes, leading to widespread grief.

In the above case, the clinical fellow may have some liability for the negligent act of the resident, and will be liable for the negligent supervision of that resident. The staff doctor will be involved in the matter as being the physician of record for the admission. Actual liability for the staff physician will depend on her knowledge of the event, written procedures, usual processes followed under these circumstances, etc.

Supervisory issues commonly arise in the following situations:

Teaching Hospitals

If you are (or ever were) an intern, resident, fellow, or staff physician in a teaching facility, did you stop to consider the extent of your liability? Most physicians don't. The case outlined in the previous section is just one of many examples where each link in the "food chain" of medical training can be included in a lawsuit. In actuality, it is not quite as brutal as it sounds – you won't be left hanging out to dry alone.

The training program bears a large portion of the supervisory responsibility (and will likely be named the primary defendant in any lawsuit).

Physician Extenders

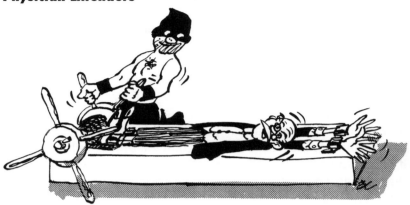

This quaint term is most frequently used to describe physician assistants and nurse practitioners who provide either primary or specialized care in a practice setting.

The number of "extenders" has been increasing significantly in recent years. These allied health professionals can significantly improve the efficiency and value (while maintaining the quality) of an organization when:

- They practice within their scope of training
- They practice within their level of experience
- They are assigned care for the appropriate patient populations

The primary caveat is to ensure that you are aware of the full range of supervisory responsibilities you have been assigned. Written policies must be followed – if you have a detailed procedure you say that you follow – and then don't – you will have a hard time defending your actions in court. Keep documentation simple, but make it clear (e.g. who does what, who reports to whom, when does the supervisee have bottom line authority, etc.).

Supervisory relationships can entail unique risks in mental health practice. Frequently there is a continuum of trained professionals providing services to patients. The training and supervisory roles vary between psychiatrists, Ph.D. psychologists, M.A. psychologists, social workers, etc. The problems that arise in this context are frequently due to a lack of understanding of exact supervisory responsibilities, or a lack of communication, or both.

A situation that commonly arises involves physicians who are assigned as physician assistant/nurse practitioner supervisors, and either have no knowledge of what this entails, or respond with indifference to this responsibility. Most state boards of professional regulation clearly delineate the degree of independence and supervision that should be present in practices with non-physician providers. The medical staff bylaws and policies of your organization will also address these relationships. As with all else, ignorance is no defense.

Caveat
Always read something before you sign it. It will not go well during a deposition if you state something like the following:

- "Um. . . er. . . Yes, that is my signature, but I didn't really read the progress note by the P.A."

- "Uh, yes, the note does state the patient has an allergy to penicillin."

- "Yes, I . . .er. . .ordered the IV ampicillin that preceded the patient's cardiac arrest by 10 minutes."

In these instances, everyone from the insurance company to the board of directors will be quite happy to settle the lawsuit without losing the farm.

Organizational Communication

Problems in organizational communication can be categorized as follows:

- Lack of established policies and procedures (this is common in smaller practices)

- Lack of awareness of policies and procedures (such as not providing orientation for the new staff supervisors or supervisees)

- Failure to execute established procedures

- Failure to use good judgment

- Failure to remember the provision of health care is a service industry

An unfortunate (but nevertheless common) example of poor communication is given in the following example:

1. A patient (who needs a walker) drives around the parking lot for fifteen minutes and cannot find a handicapped parking spot (the one available spot is filled). She then parks in a no parking zone.

2. The parking expedition has made her ten minutes late for her appointment. She is brusquely chastised at the check-in window (without being given a chance to explain). She then waits 40 minutes to see the doctor (with no explanation or apology for the delay).

3. After spending only 12 minutes with the doctor, she is given a prescription at the pharmacy, which she believes is incorrect (since no one explained that a generic substitution was given in place of her usual medication).

4. After waiting another 20 minutes to speak with the pharmacist, she goes to see the patient contact representative to tell him about the problems she's encountered. No one is available, only a sign saying "back in ten minutes."

5. Upon leaving, in a state of exasperation, she notices she now has a ticket on her car!

6. The administrator of the facility never hears about any of these problems, and has no opportunity to intervene. Eventually a curt letter of complaint arrives from the EEOC regarding the inadequate number of handicapped parking spots (there are formulas in place based on the number of patient visits and other variables).

7. The patient just happens to be on the board of directors for one of the companies having a contract with the healthcare organization. The contract isn't renewed. Everyone suffers – the patient with the bad experience, the lost opportunities the organization had for making improvements, and the loss of market share.

Caveat

For every one person who has a bad experience and tells you about it, there are at least 20 others who didn't tell you. However, you can be certain that every friend and acquaintance will have heard about it.

Physicians tend to be oblivious to many of the above occurrences, but it is important that you and your patients know how to address the many small things that can happen during each visit.

Although you may not have control over every aspect of a patient's unhappy experience, if there is an unfavorable outcome, you may take the brunt of the blame. It's not fair, but it's reality. For this reason, it is recommended that you have one or two staff members who have excellent interpersonal skills, and who can help fix the little things upon which your patients judge much of their experience.

Credentialing and Privileging

These two terms are frequently used interchangeably. It is important to understand the differences, and the potential issues related to each action.

Credentialing Physicians

In most organizations, **credentialing** refers to the collection and review of information about a physician's background. This information is important when an organization is considering a physician for a clinical position. **Privileging** is the actual granting of privileges for work in that setting. This may or may not be included in the credentialing process. The actual process is addressed in the bylaws of the organization. There are several different levels of privilege that will be defined by individual organizations.

The credentialing process should be tailored to the specific organization and clearly delineated in writing. There are several formal components of a credentials file, which may include the following:

- Education (undergraduate and medical school)
- Training (internship, residency, fellowship)
- Licensure
- Board Certification(s)
- References and Recommendations
- Query of NPDB (hospitals *must* query initially and every two years; other organizations may query)
- Other training (e.g. ACLS or PALS certification)

The physician being considered for privileges should always be asked to sign a release of information for the above information. A prudent credentialing process will ensure verification of the submitted material with the original source (i.e. verification from the state board of licensure instead of only a copy of the physicians license).

Even the smallest organization should have some mechanism for review and approval of physicians' credentials. The JCAHO, NCQA, and federal and state laws also provide guidelines for credentialing processes.

Potential areas of liability are as follows:

- Negligent credentialing, which is the failure to adequately screen an applicant who goes on to cause subsequent injury to a patient (remember the "deep pockets" approach to litigation)

- Failure to obtain proper releases; if damaging information about the physician is released without his consent, it can place the organization at risk for legal action

- Violating laws (such as ADA); requesting disclosure of information regarding physical/mental disorders during the credentialing process can be hazardous

- Economic credentialing is the use of data in the credentialing process which predicts the physician's financial impact on the organization, rather than on evidence of training, ability and skill level (this is a definite no-no, and is further discussed in this chapter)

Credentialing Allied Health Professionals
Allied health professionals (AHP) include several types of providers: physician assistants, nurse practitioners, nurse midwives, nurse anesthetists, clinical psychologists, physical

therapists, optometrists, podiatrists, social workers, etc. Any organization employing AHPs needs to have a clearly defined, class-specific credentialing process. The type of information sought is often similar to that for credentialing physicians. The privileges granted to AHPs must be very clearly delineated and include the following parameters:

- *Scope of Practice* – this is dependent on state law in many cases and should be tailored to the needs of the organization

- *Level of Supervision* – this too needs to be clearly delineated for each class of provider, and based on state law and the scope of practice authorized; a supervisor needs to be clearly assigned

- *Prescribing Authority* – this is also based on state law

Economic Credentialing

This is a relatively recent consideration. Most MCOs have some means to compare the practice activities of the physicians providing service under their contracts or employment. This is typically called **physician profiling**. Some of this data is fairly innocuous and is geared to providing information and indicators regarding how well physicians meet the quality standards compared with other health care organizations, etc. For example, with the **Health Plan Employer Data and Information Set (HEDIS)** measures are collected on all managed care plans. This information must be submitted by organizations evaluated by the **National Committee for Quality Assurance (NCQA)**. This information may include the percentage of children vaccinated, number of women who receive breast cancer screening, the percentage of prenatal care provided for first-trimester mothers, the percentage of patients questioned about seatbelt use, etc. This information provides reviewers with an idea about the general effectiveness of preventive measures. What is disconcerting is that data is collected on physicians for things like the number of referrals made to specialists, the number of tests ordered, choice of non-formulary drugs prescribed, frequency of follow-up visits, length of visits, etc.

The natural sequence of events has resulted in these data being used when hiring or firing physicians. Some doctors have been fired ("deselected") because of their practice activities. It is not appropriate to undertake a negative privileging action based on economic credentialing.

Organizations have the right to deselect a physician if there is a clause in the contract which specifies reasons for dismissal (and this is followed). Using fiscal performance as a credentialing criterion is not allowed. Deselection may be done as an employment action, *not* as a privileging action. Physicians have the right to take legal action if economic credentialing was used against them.

Caveat
Always review your employment contract with a knowledgeable lawyer. Read your medical staff bylaws and ask to review your credentials file.

Contracts
Never sign a contract without reviewing it with a lawyer familiar with managed care issues. Many a physician has signed a contract that looked fair, and then learned the hard way about the "small print" or the unusual phraseology contained in the last few paragraphs.

Caveat
What the large print provideth, the fine print taketh away.

Reviewing your contract with a lawyer is not an act of bad faith. Instead, it demonstrates that you are someone who makes decisions based on the best possible information (which demonstrates your good judgment). Review the contract for the "gag clauses." These are always unethical, and increasingly illegal in many jurisdictions.

Caveat
An organization will transfer as much risk to physicians as they possibly can.

You need to know if the organization can "deselect" you for any reason, or if they must demonstrate just cause.

You also want to be aware of any restrictions on your practice should you choose to leave the organization (or your contract is not renewed). Several rueful doctors can attest to learning about the "non-compete" clauses in their contracts which restricted them from practicing within 50 miles of their original place of employment for five years (after they purchased their dream home and paid tuition for their children's private schools).

There are also things called **hold harmless clauses** which provide the MCO with an additional shield from liability.

There are many other subtle issues that can arise in employment contracts. They can quickly be identified by a good contract lawyer who specializes in healthcare law (or at least has significant practice experience in this area – don't hesitate to ask). This is not the time to go to Uncle Fudd who has a general law practice and will give you a freebie. Pay now for the expertise, or (perhaps) pay dearly, later.

Caveat
Never bolt your door with a boiled carrot.

Irish Proverb

Other Liabilities

Responsibilities follow membership in any organization. Some of these responsibilities are the ones that come with your profession (these are the easy ones). Many others are related to the organization and policies set by both internal and external authorities. Major areas of organizational liability include:

Knowing Your Organization's Policies and Procedures

Every new staff member should receive a full orientation (which can last up to three days or longer). For a variety of reasons, orientations for physicians are often overlooked (e.g. they are too busy, their time is perceived as being too valuable to "waste" on a routine orientation, they are needed for patient care, etc.). This turns into a big problem when the physician turns out to be the only member of the organization who truly is unaware of his rights and responsibilities. For example, if the physician files a lawsuit against the organization for sexual harassment or discrimination, and was not given a thorough orientation (and annual update), the organization may well be held liable.

If the physician does not take the time to understand her responsibilities as a member of the medical staff, she could be liable for not undertaking a required action (e.g. mandatory reporting of an impaired colleague). She could end up losing her privileges, facing an action from the state board of licensure, and having a report made to the NPDB.

Suggestions for avoiding these consequences are as follows:

- Know your supervisory responsibilities

- Be aware of the non-clinical responsibilities that affect your practice. These are things like ensuring that your staff and patients have a safe working environment. Even with a small practice that is not held to JCAHO (or similar) standards, you still have a responsibility to attend to the things that a lay person would consider important (e.g. poor lighting, slippery floors, pot holes in the parking lot, etc.).

• Be aware of any potential gaps in your current professional liability insurance – particularly if you are changing coverage, or are taking on additional duties that are not usually covered in traditional medical malpractice insurance policies (like involvement in peer review activities or board activities).

References

Bernstein BE, Hartsell TL: *The Portable Lawyer for Mental Health Professionals*.
John Wiley and Sons, Inc., N.Y., 1998

Gutheil T: *Supervisor, Supervisee, and Medical Backup.*
The Mental Health Practitioner and the Law.
Harvard University Press, 1998

Reid WH: **Impaired Colleagues**.
Journal of Practical Psychiatry and Behavioral Health, 291-293, 1999

Vasile RG, Gutheil TG: **The Psychiatrist as Medical Backup?: Ambiguity in the Delegation of Clinical Responsibility**.
American Journal of Psychiatry 136: 1292-1296, 1979

Zaremski MJ: **Peer Review Immunity Upheld by Federal Appeals Court**.
American Medical News Oct 4:13, 1999

9. Issues Related to Medical Specialties

This chapter presents some of the issues, regulations, difficult situations, and liabilities that apply primarily to certain medical specialties. This chapter is not meant to provide comprehensive guidelines for each specialty.

While obstetricians have one of the highest rates of malpractice claims of any specialty, they also have the greatest knowledge of the primary liabilities in their practices. The specialties addressed in this chapter are:

- Emergency Medicine
- Psychiatry
- Pediatrics/Perinatalolgy
- Plastic Surgery
- Pathology
- General Practice

Emergency Medicine
Antidumping Legislation
The ER is a potential legal minefield because it encompasses so many high-risk elements (no ongoing relationship with the patient, increased risk of a bad outcome, etc.). There are also state and federal "antidumping" laws. As presented in Chapter 8, EMTALA prohibits an ER from denying patients an evaluation for, and stabilization of, their emergent medical problems.

Recent legislation in several states (and the proposed Patient Bill of Rights) addresses the competing concerns of federal law requiring a medical screening exam, against the preauthorization required by many MCOs. Only "reasonable" delays are allowed in these circumstances.

Specialty Care

Pediatric cases are another huge area of potential litigation for ER physicians. Many of the cases seen in urgent situations involve children with fevers. In most instances, the fever is due to a self-limiting cause (usually a viral illness), that requires only supportive treatment. Notwithstanding, a missed case of meningitis or encephalitis is every physician's nightmare. It is not appropriate to do a full work-up on every patient, but it is important to consider a full differential diagnosis, and act accordingly. The majority of successful malpractice lawsuits involving febrile children are complicated cases, and are not solely based on an unfavorable outcome. Some of the problems noted in these cases are:

- An inadequate period of evaluation

- An inadequately documented physical exam

- Poor instructions upon discharge

- A lack of consideration (and documentation) of more serious causes of fevers

False Imprisonment

False imprisonment is an issue for many departments in a hospital. As discussed previously, competent adults can refuse treatment, even if it is life-saving.

Informed Consent

Obtaining IC may be overlooked for a variety of reasons: the emergent nature of the illness, the lack of time to fully cover the required elements, the lack of training of staff, etc. Of all possible reasons, it is most likely the attitude of ER staff that IC is not required in an "emergency." Depending on the ER, the actual acuity of patients who present for evaluation and treatment varies widely. In an inner-city location with a high percentage of trauma victims, ensuring that patients give proper IC may not be the highest priority (nor should it be when seconds count). In other settings, the "emergency exception" to IC should be applied much less frequently. Again, federal law (EMTALA) defines an emergency medical condition as: *A medical condition that manifests itself by acute symptoms of sufficient severity, including severe pain, such that the absence of immediate medical attention could reasonably be expected to result in placing the health of the individual in serious jeopardy.*

However, unless someone is comatose, or a delay of a few minutes would clearly cause harm, you should always attempt to obtain IC from the patient (or guardian). Basic IC for a screening evaluation can be assumed from the fact the patient presented to the ER. Past the basics, however, patients in the ER have the same right to IC (and refusal of further evaluation or treatment) as they do when being treated in less acute settings.

Remember that obtaining IC from ER patients involves an understanding of their diagnosis, the risks and benefits of the proposed intervention and of alternative interventions, and likely consequences of receiving no intervention.

On Call Liability
What happens when the on-call physician declines to evaluate or take responsibility for a patient after being contacted by the ER? There have been several cases where a medical negligence lawsuit was filed for exactly this reason.

There are two issues in these cases. The first is whether or not the physician can be successfully sued for medical negligence.

The courts have been split on this issue, even at the appellate level. The question is whether the on-call physician has a *duty* to the patient, and breaches this duty by refusing to come to evaluate the patient. Secondly, most organizations have addressed this issue in writing, found either in the physician's contract or in the medical staff bylaws. A breach of either of these situations can result in adverse privileging actions, being deselected from the organization, or being sued by the organization for breach of contract, etc.

Psychiatry

The main problems that lead to malpractice lawsuits against psychiatrists include:

- Misdiagnosis
- Medication related problems
- Failure to provide adequate treatment
- Failure to obtain informed consent
- Sexual misconduct,
- Failure to protect patients from self-harm
- Failure to protect others (duties to third parties)
- Violation of confidentiality

Note that psychotherapy is not in the above list. Psychiatrists don't get sued for providing poor therapy – because no one knows what good therapy is! While this is a somewhat cynical overgeneralization, there have been very few lawsuits that allege negligent psychotherapy. Fewer still are successful. The reason for this relative freedom from lawsuits, is that psychotherapy:

- Makes no physical intervention

- Can rarely be held accountable for an unfavorable outcome (i.e. it is difficult to prove a connection between a lousy interpretation and a subsequent negative event)

The last point may sound a bit tongue-in-cheek, but it is very difficult to establish reliable outcome indicators or SOC for the numerous types of psychotherapy (e.g psychodynamic, cognitive-behavioral). The few successful cases involving negligent psychotherapy have been *res ipsa loquitor* cases.

Psychiatrists do get sued for a variety of other things that may or may not relate to the quality of the therapy they provide.

Mental health professionals have the best and the worst situation when it comes to ethics and law. There are numerous guidelines dictating what constitutes *professional behavior* during psychotherapy, as well as stringent requirements for the highest level of moral conduct. Most psychiatrists are made aware of these requirements through their training and specialty societies.

Additionally, psychiatry has an entire subspecialty devoted to the application of psychiatric training and experience to issues in legal settings. All psychiatry residents receive some exposure to forensic psychiatry during training, and are often better prepared to deal with legal and ethical issues because of this experience.

Several excellent references regarding the many ethical and medicolegal issues in mental health practices are included at the end of this chapter. A few areas that can be considered "hotspots" are as follows:

Negligent Psychotherapy

As mentioned above, it is very difficult to be successfully sued for negligent psychotherapy. This happens mainly when a psychotherapist is practicing a form of therapy with little or no peer-reviewed endorsement, or is behaving in a blatantly unprofessional manner. There have been some outrageous things done in the name of "therapy." Usually this involves physical contact, and in one particularly egregious case, was called "tickle therapy."

One of the well-known cases in psychiatry revolved around a claim of negligence, which principally alleged a lack of IC. Ultimately, the case was settled out of court, and for this reason sets no legal precedent. Still, the details are of educational value.

In 1984, a physician was admitted to a psychiatric hospital and treated with psychoanalytic therapy for a severe, agitated depression. After several months with no improvement, he was transferred to another hospital, received antidepressant medication, and within a short period of time improved significantly. He began to question why he wasn't offered medication at the first treatment facility, and brought forth a lawsuit. A malpractice tribunal awarded him $250,000.

Caveat

You cannot limit treatment to the type offered by you or your institution. Patients must be provided with information regarding all alternative treatments (with their risks and benefits).

A recent case followed closely by all psychiatrists involved Dr. Myron Liptzin. The jury awarded $500,000 to the plaintiff, Wendell Williamson, a former University of North Carolina Law student. He saw Dr. Liptzin for a total of six visits. What is unusual about this case is that Williamson was found to be not guilty by reason of insanity (NGRI) when he stopped taking his antipsychotic medication – and later shot and killed two people while wounding a third. Although there are several issues in this case, the two significant take away points for psychiatrists are:

- Ensure your patients have the names of *specific* physicians for them to see when you retire or move

- If your patient agrees, contact their support system, and instruct them on what to do in the event of a psychiatric emergency

Suicide

The primary areas of litigation involving psychiatrists are: assessing of suicidal risk (and other forms of violence), and the use of psychotropic medications. A rule of thumb is that 50% of inpatient suicides will result in a malpractice claim. Whether or not the case is successful depends on documentation, particularly regarding your decision-making process during the hospitalization.

It is surprising how many psychiatrists fail to document their RA for suicidal patients, particularly when changes in the level of supervision are made. For example, if you take a patient off ward restriction, and he commits suicide at the first opportunity, your medical records should provide a clear indication about why you decreased the level of observation.

Psychiatrists are more frequently sued for inpatient suicides than for outpatient. This is because it is believed that there is a greater responsibility to keep the patient safe (since she was ill enough to need hospitalization).

A malpractice suit of concern to non-psychiatric physicians involves a patient who committed suicide, with subsequent legal action being brought by her parents. In this case, the patient killed herself with a prescription supplied by the primary care doctor. Luckily, he had a well-documented MSE at the time of the last visit. She clearly knew her options for treatment, had refused hospitalization, and exhibited few risk factors for suicide (at the time of the appointment). The Illinois Supreme Court sided with the trial court (overthrowing the appellate court's decision), and stated that the patient carried responsibility for her actions (contributory negligence). The court cited a state civil code in which an individual has a duty to exercise ordinary care for her own safety.

The concern voiced by many physicians in this case was that even in the absence of any evidence of negligence, they could still be held liable because a patient committed suicide while under their care. Never is the need for clear documentation of a thoughtful RA more important than in the evaluation of dangerousness of an individual to self and others. There are many excellent books and courses taught on this subject.

Other grounds for lawsuits are often not due to medical negligence, but for civil (and criminal) areas such as breach of confidentiality, false imprisonment, and sexual misconduct.

Sexual Misconduct

This topic was presented in Chapter 4. While some mental health professionals dispute the "perpetuity rule," a prudent therapist would not. The American Psychiatry Association states this in its code of ethics. Dr. Woody (1997) put this nicely in his book: *"Once a client, always a client. At the risk of seeming impolite, if a therapist cannot find social or romantic companions from other than a pool of persons to whom the therapist has provided treatment, perhaps he or she should seek professional help."*

Recovered Memories

A hot topic in the 1990's was that of recovered memories (and related lawsuits). This issue has become so liability laden that there are several professional negligence insurance companies who refuse to provide coverage for recovered memory treatment.

The first case to make major headlines was that of Gary Ramona, who sued his daughter's therapists in 1994, and was awarded $500,000. He alleged that negligent psychotherapy implanted false memories of child sexual abuse. The court stated that the therapists incurred a duty to Gary Ramona when they encouraged his daughter to confront him. This was the first time a non-patient family member was allowed to seek damages in this type of case. The court's finding raised concern in the psychiatric community about similar cases and duties to third parties.

A more recent, and well-publicized recovered memory case, occurred in 1997 when a patient sued her psychiatrist directly. The settlement was for $10.75 million dollars. There were allegations of negligent care, this time occurring over a six-year period, and involving recovered memories of satanic ritual abuse. The psychiatrist is now suing the insurance company.

The majority of court findings indicate that arguments related to the establishment of duty to a third party are more easily *disproven* than *proven*. Such cases ask the court to find that a duty existed (where normally one did not), and to hold a healthcare professional responsible to an individual for having provided negligent treatment to someone else.

Caveat
Maintaining neutrality is crucial – do not dispense advice about what patients should or shouldn't do in their relationships. Instead, help the patient come to his own conclusions and make his own decisions.

Since the first recovered memories cases were filed in the 1980's, more than 800 have been brought forth. Interestingly, however, these claims are slowing in frequency.

The major reason for this is that the **Daubert standard** is now required for expert testimony. This standard requires that the substance of expert testimony be based on scientific principles, requiring that a process demonstrate a reproducible rate of error (among other things). A theory that cannot be tested, or have its rate of error established, cannot be accepted as "scientific" in nature.

Prior to 1993, the **Frye test** was the standard, requiring general acceptance in the scientific community. In recovered memories cases, the allegations were based on negligent care, and as noted previously, it is almost impossible to prove a deviation from the SOC if there isn't one for a procedure or technique. It is difficult to find scientific support for the theory of repressed memories, even though this concept is accepted (at least to some degree) by many practitioners. **Repression** is indirectly addressed in the DSM-IV section on **dissociative disorders**.

Misdiagnosis

Psychiatrists should be aware that a percentage of their patients have an underlying medical disorder as the cause of their psychiatric symptom(s). The chapter by Gold (1998), referenced at the end of this chapter, is an excellent summary. Many studies indicate that 5-10% of psychiatric outpatients have medical disorders that produce mental, emotional, or behavioral symptoms.

Some interesting statistics on the medical causes of psychiatric symptoms are as follows:

- 46% of patients referred to psychiatric services suffer from one or more undiagnosed medical disorders

- Medical personnel failed to find 32% of physical illnesses present in patients referred to them

- Psychiatrists failed to find 48% of physical illnesses present in patients referred to them

- 83% of patients self-referred, or sent by social agencies, had an undetected physical illness at time of their outpatient evaluation

- Less than 35% of psychiatrists give their patients a physical examination

- 91 medical disorders can present with symptoms of depression

- 24 medical disorders frequently induce depression

If psychiatrists at least consider the possibility that their patients are suffering from an underlying medical illness, they will be more likely to diagnose and treat these conditions.

You do not need to get wrapped around the axle searching for "zebras" (rare medical conditions) – just consider the possibility. Once again, a concise, well-written note indicating that you at least considered (and did basic screening for) a medical condition before making a psychiatric diagnosis, will suffice.

Caveat
You are allowed to make errors of judgment (taking one reasoned choice over another), but not errors of fact (not considering other, reasonable possibilities).

Record Keeping
Mental health professionals are cautioned to keep their records indefinitely. Check your state laws for specific guidelines on the length of time that you must keep your records (typical ranges are from 3 to 10 years). Sometimes, a party looking for a scapegoat for a failed marriage/job may point a finger at the therapy that he, or someone else, received.

Pediatrics/Perinatology

Pediatricians who have an active perinatal practice, like obstetricians, tend to be quite aware of the hotspots in their practices. An important issue with pediatric cases is the wisdom in keeping medical records beyond the required time period. Most state laws word the statute of limitations for medical negligence as "X years from the injury, or from when the patient reasonably should have known of the injury." The latter period of time referred to in this definition may be quite a bit longer than X (which is usually 2 or 3 years). Many states allow a lawsuit to be brought as late as age eleven. A period of hypoxia, or a pediatric misdiagnosis, around the time of birth may have obvious manifestations for several years.

Plastic Surgery

This specialty frequently experiences several legal risks, such as IC, breach of contract, and safety in the anesthesia and post-op time frame. A conservative policy about operating on patients who are smokers is also prudent. High-risk areas for plastic surgeons include the following:

Procedures Performed in Office Surgical Suites

- Ensure good preoperative screening to identify those patients with higher medical risks (and perform procedures on these patients in hospital settings)

- Ensure impeccable procedures for credentialing of the anesthesiologists and nurse-anesthetists.

- Document proper preventive maintenance on all equipment (this is your responsibility in an office practice)

Smoking

- Be aware that many avoidable claims are directly related to complications caused by smoking

- If the patient is a heavy smoker, consider declining or postponing the procedure

- Ensure you have documented that the patient was warned of the risks if she continues to smoke after the procedure (e.g. sloughs, poor healing, resultant scars)

- Postpone surgery for at least one month after the nonsmoking period begins, and have the patient sign an affidavit (you can check for nicotine in urine if doubts arise)

Obtain Detailed Photographs

- These can be instrumental in your defense; get them both before and after surgery

Informed Consent

- In addition to your usual discussion about the risks and benefits for any procedure, ensure patients also understand the psychological risks and benefits, and have realistic expectations (record any questions in your progress notes); use the "tummy test" – if your gut tells you the patient just doesn't quite get it, you are better off not performing the surgery (don't rationalize away your doubts – they exist for good reasons)

• If your patient is a medical person, don't assume he understands the routine – spell it out as you would for anyone

• If your patient needs a translator, ensure one is available, particularly someone who is highly skilled and can truly explain nuances; do not use a family member or friend

Patient Selection Criteria
• When reviewed by another surgeon after an unfavorable outcome, many cases showed that the operating surgeon had doubts about the patient's suitability for the procedure, but went against her better judgment

Pathology

This specialty may seem to be an odd one to include in a list of high-risk situations. Given the Bad Outcome/Bad Feelings formula for litigation, the pathologist usually doesn't get involved until after the damage has been done.

The area of practice that causes about 40% of all malpractice claims against pathologists involves Pap smears. As with any test, there are always false negative readings. Unfortunately, the general expectation for Pap smears is that they detect all cancers, and do so in the early stages. Malpractice suits resulting from these false expectations have caused many institutions to recommend that all patients be provided with accurate information, and sign an IC form prior to the procedure. As with everything else, a patient who understands the limitations of Pap smears will not be surprised at a reasonably foreseeable, unfavorable outcome.

Treatment Refusal Forms
There are many generic forms used for this purpose. They should contain what the basics of an IC form includes, plus a section detailing the risks of refusing the procedure. Remember the *Truman v. Thomas* case in the discussion about IC? If Dr. Thomas had used one of these forms, he might have been found not guilty.

General Practice
General practitioners face many potential sources of liability. Three main ones are presented here. Remember, as part of your RM plan, brainstorm with your colleagues regarding which are your top ten risks, and focus your efforts accordingly.

Breast Cancer Assessments
Malpractice suits related to the diagnosis of breast cancer are the most common, and most costly of all cancer-related suits. They are the second most common reason that medical malpractice suits are initiated. With 180,000 new cases last year,

and 44,000 deaths, there is a good reason that it is the most feared of all diagnoses (even though more women die from lung cancer and even more from heart disease).

Many physicians ignore the many well-established procedures in the proper assessment of breast cancer. They may also overlook those women in high-risk categories (family history, history of radiation treatment to thorax, prior history of one breast cancer, history of meningioma, age, post menopausal status, etc.). Some physicians minimize breast symptoms when reported by young women.

If you evaluate women as part of your practice, ensure that you conduct a thorough work-up. Remember, the mammogram is a diagnostic aid, with a false negative rate of 5-20%. The *only* reliable means of correct diagnosis is by invasive tissue diagnosis.

Colorectal Cancer

This area of practice has been, and will continue to be, a major cause of medical malpractice suits. Recommendations involving this illness are:

- Ensure you follow an accepted process for the evaluation of possible colorectal cancer, either developed by your specialty society, or one published in a peer-reviewed journal for primary care physicians. Although clinical guidelines do not establish the SOC by themselves, they do provide up-to-date guidelines that are based on the best practice data, and will ensure you are consistent in your evaluations.

- Never just assume the cause of occult bleeding is a previously diagnosed ulcer (or any other "knee-jerk" diagnosis). Similarly, never assume the cause of bright red blood on the toilet paper is always from hemorrhoids. The number one reason for malpractice actions is the failure to obtain an appropriate endoscopic exam. In cases where the patient is reticent, consider use of a treatment refusal form, if, after a thorough discussion, this procedure is still refused.

• Take a thorough history. Clearly delineate and characterize the symptoms you are addressing, and clearly document your decision-making process. Note whether there is a positive or negative family history.

• Unless you are absolutely sure of the quality of the radiographic exam you order, review the results (particularly abnormal ones) with the radiologist to see the situation for yourself.

Depression and the Elderly

Many articles draw attention to the under-diagnosis of depression in the elderly, and the inadequate treatment provided. A closely related concern is the marked increase in suicide risk in this population. Many factors contribute to this situation:

• Physicians may spend less time with older patients

• Lack of attribution of physical symptoms to a mood or anxiety disorder

• Lack of current knowledge regarding recommended treatments, etc.

All elderly patients should be screened for depression, and if it is discovered, it should be treated promptly. This screening process can be part of the comprehensive **biopsychosocial assessment** performed on patients. If there is any evidence of depression, the person must be asked (in a very matter of fact way) about their thoughts of suicide. This can be queried as follows: *"Many people who are going through what you're experiencing with your (loss, pain, cancer etc.), have thoughts about hurting themselves or that life isn't worth living anymore. Have you had thoughts like this?"*

Find wording that you are comfortable with and that doesn't seem abrupt, insensitive, or "out of the blue" to patients. Avoid leading questions such as *"You haven't been having any thoughts of hurting yourself, have you?"* This approach will shut the patient down very quickly. Ideally, patients should be as comfortable telling you about their thoughts of self-harm as they are their coughs, sniffles, and bowel habits.

References

Behnke SH: **Old Duties and New: Recovered Memories and the Question of Third Party Liability**.
J Am Acad Psychiatry and the Law 27:279-300, 1999

Bernstein BE, Hartsell TL:
The Portable Lawyer for Mental Health Professionals.
John Wiley and Sons, Inc. N.Y. 1998

Bongar B, Berman AL, Maris RW et al: **Risk Management with Suicidal Patients**.
The Guilford Press, New York City, 1998

Bozeman FC: **On-Call Physician Liability to Emergency Room Patients**.
Escambia County Medical Society Bulletin May:5, 1999

Daubert v. Merril Dow Pharmaceuticals, Inc. 113 S.Ct. 2786 (1993)

Flach F (ed): **Malpractice Risk Management in Psychiatry**.
Hatherleigh Press, New York, 1998

Frye v. US, 293 F.1013 [1923]

Gold MS: *The Risk of Misdiagnosing Physical Illness as Depression.*
Malpractice Risk Management in Psychiatry.
Hatherleigh Press, Inc. NY 1998

Medicolegal Issues in Clinical Practice

Gorney M, Martello J: **The Genesis of Plastic Surgeon Claims – A Review of Recurring Problems**.
Clinics in Plastic Surgery 26:123-131, 1999

Grinfeld MJ: **Recovered Memory Lawsuit Sparks Litigation**.
Psychiatric Times 16(12):1,3-4, 1999

Gutheil TG, Gabbard GO: **The Concept of Boundaries in Clinical Practice: Theoretical and Risk Management Dimensions**.
Am J Psych 150:188-196, 1993

Harshberger KE: **Informed Consent and the Pap Smear: Avoiding Malpractice Through Information**.
Legal Medicine 99:42, 1999

Hausman K: **Jury Faults Psychiatrist For Murder By Ex-Patient**.
Psychiatric News Nov 6:1,22, 1998

Illinois Psychiatrists Help Win Court Victory.
Psychiatric Times 34(3):1,22, 1999

Johnson LJ: **Avoiding Lawsuits About Colorectal Cancer**.
Medical Economics, Aug 11, 1997. www.pdr.net/memag, accessed 12/3/99

Kaplan MS, Adamek ME, Calderon A: **Managing Depressed and Suicidal Geriatric Patients: Differences Among Primary Care Physicians**.
Gerontologist 39:417-125, 1999

Lief HI: **Patient Versus Therapist: Legal Actions Over Recovered Memory Therapy**.
Psychiatric Times Nov: 36-39, 1999

Lifson LE and Simon RI, ed:
The Mental Health Practitioner and the Law.
Harvard Univ Press, Boston, 1998

Oscheroff v. Chestnut Lodge, 304 MD. 163,, 497 A2d 1163 (1985)

Palmer RM: **Geriatric Assessment**.
Med Clin North Am 83:1503-23, 1999

Perlin ML: *A Comprehensive Guide to Malpractice Risk Management in Psychiatry*. **Risk Issues In Psychiatric Malpractice**.
Heatherleigh Press, NY, 1999

Slovenko R: **Legal Duties of Therapists to Third Parties**.
Psychiatric Times Aug:51-52, 1999

Thewes MA, Fitzgerald D, Sulmasy DP: **Informed Consent in Emergency Medicine – Ethics Under Fire**.
Emergency Med Clin of NA 14:245-254, 1996

Weiss RB: **Breast Disease Diagnoses: Making the Same Old Errors, Over and Over Again**.
Legal Medicine 99:19, 1999

Woody RH: *Legally Safe Mental Health Practice – Psycholegal Questions And Answers*.
Psychosocial Press, Madison CT, 1997

Zimmerly JG: **Medical Legal Issues in the Evaluation of the Febrile Pediatric Patient**.
Legal Medicine 99:30, 1999

10. Odds & Ends

This chapter contains information that doesn't quite fit with the topics presented in other chapters. Also included is a section offering solutions to common practice problems, and a section outlining "tools" to deal with several high-risk situations.

Conflicts of Interest

Potential conflicts of interest were discussed in the Boundary Issues section of Chapter 4, the Other Ethical Issues section in Chapter 6, and again in Chapter 7. For psychiatrists, the mantra for staying clear of conflicts of interest is "once a patient, always a patient." Physicians from all areas of medicine would be well served by adhering to this principle. You will avoid potential conflicts of interest if you ensure that you do not put yourself in a position to gain financially or personally from your relationship with a patient (current or former). This means: no stock tips (insider trading), no business partnerships, no close friendships – just professional relationships. The intrinsic satisfaction you get from providing quality medical care is all the benefit you can safely get (and should need) from dealing with patients. Period.

The Sale of Products From Your Office

A recent debate within the AMA centered on the practice of

selling medical products from professional offices. The "pro" argument for this practice is that the patient should have the option to purchase the "best" products for their various conditions (be they facial creams, vitamins, etc.). By offering these products to the patient in your office, you are theoretically helping the patient. If you sell the product at cost (that is, no profit), no potential conflict of interest exists. The "con" argument is that patients may feel coerced into purchasing these products from their physicians. This (potential) sense of coercion results from the imbalance of power, control, and authority, which is inherent in the DPR. This issue is particularly important if you stand to profit from patients' purchases. This issue is no different than referring patients to facilities (in which you have a financial interest) for medical tests. Rather than find a way rationalize this activity, your safest option is to avoid putting yourself in an ethically compromised position.

Caveat
To be on the ethical high ground, you need to tell patients whenever you stand to gain something (monetarily or otherwise) from decisions involving their care.

The current guidelines from the AMA Council on Ethical and Judicial Affairs reiterate the above recommendations. If you do decide to sell products in your office, the following three requirements should be met:

- No profit is to be made from selling these items
- No semblance of coercion should enter the process
- Full disclosure of the financial incentives must be made

Gifts From Pharmaceutical Companies
This continues to be a hot topic because of the potential to influence physicians' prescribing practices. A further concern is that the costs of these initiatives are simply passed onto patients. Pharmaceutical companies don't spend millions of dollars on gifts yearly out of sheer gratitude.

The more that a pharmaceutical company stands to gain from any gift or service, the more stringent you need to be in accepting its offers. Further, the more authority you have in an organization, the greater is the potential for "undue influence" over your decisions. The safest practice for medical directors and Vice-Presidents of Medical Affairs (VPMA) is to accept no gifts worth more than $5.

The AMA Council on Ethical and Judicial Affairs developed guidelines for this area. Their recommendation is that gifts must be of modest value (absolutely under $100), and provide some benefit to patients. Many organizations have policies that are much more conservative. For example, an organization might dictate that no gift from an industry can be accepted if its value is greater than $20, with a limit of $50 per year. The intent of this restriction is to avoid any influence on the purchaser/prescriber, and to remove any perception of impropriety. These limitations also apply to other industries, such as medical supply companies, equipment suppliers, etc.

There is widespread agreement that inexpensive items that may benefit patients are acceptable (e.g. pens, patient information kits, some textbooks, etc.).

Caveat

A conflict of interest is *not* an ethical dilemma. A **conflict of interest** places one set of values over another (i.e. your interests over the patient's). An **ethical dilemma** is one that has two competing values, each of which are in the best interests of patients. Ethical dilemmas may involve end of life issues, civil commitment, or issues which may pit the best interests of one patient against the best interests of another (e.g. transplant organ allocation).

Prescribing Issues

Medication errors can cause significant harm to patients. Some of the major concerns are as follows:

Legibility

In some lawsuits, the signature of the physician was enlarged to fill a five-foot long display. When the jury had the chance to stare at the exhibit for several days, they grew more and more incensed at the illegibility, and decided against the scribbling doctor.

Drug Name Similarities

Be particularly cautious when you are prescribing one drug that has a similar name to another. This is both a legibility and accuracy issue. A case in point is the similarity in the nonproprietary names of the cardiac drugs *amrinone* and *amiodarone*. The first is a vasodilator with positive inotropic action, the latter an antiarrhythmic. Confusion between these similar names has so far resulted in 11 medication errors and one death. Authorities are proposing a name change for each to avoid further morbidity.

Documentation

If it isn't documented – it didn't happen.

Informed Consent

As with any other evaluation or treatment procedure, prescribing any medication to a patient requires proper IC. This involves telling the patient the diagnosis, the risks/benefits of the recommended treatment, the risks/benefits of alternative treatments, and the risks/benefits of receiving no treatment.

The legal requirement is that the patient be made aware of her "material risks," or what the reasonable person in the same situation would want to know. This does not mean you need to discuss every possible side effect listed in the Physician's Desk Reference (PDR), only the substantial or common ones. Some jurisdictions have determined an actual percentage equating to a material risk. If your jurisdiction defines a material risk as one that occurs at least 1% of the time, then you should tell the patient about the side effects known to occur with that frequency, as well as the serious side effects that occur less often.

Medications Prescribed for a Non-FDA Approved Use

If you are using a drug in a way that is not approved by the FDA (and not noted in the PDR), you must let the patient know this. The lack of official approval does not restrict you from using the medication. Some unapproved medications are the "drug of choice" for treating certain conditions. Before using a medication in a non-approved way, be certain that you have scientific evidence and peer-reviewed articles to back your decision.

Non-FDA Approved Drugs

A variation on the above theme is the use of a non-approved medication, a situation for which extreme caution is advised. Not uncommonly, medications have been used for years in other countries, but have not received FDA approval (for any of a variety of reasons). While the use of such medications may be well supported by scientific evidence in peer-reviewed journals, it is technically against the law to use them (and difficult to defend in a lawsuit). A consent form would be advisable in situations where you intend to proceed with a non-approved medication.

Exceeding Recommended Doses (In Amount or Frequency of Administration)

The PDR is a helpful guide, but if in your opinion (and based on medical evidence), a higher (or lower) dose is appropriate, follow your clinical judgment. This situation is particularly common with the use/amount of pain medication in terminal cancer patients. Ensure proper IC is obtained and that your decisions are well documented with regard to how/why you made your decision. Do not avoid giving adequate pain relief for fear of straying from the PDR recommendations – just to be certain to document your rationale.

Controlled Substances

Be aware of, and abide by, local rules regarding schedules.

Prescribing for Yourself or Family Members

Generally, as long as you are not obtaining controlled substances, self-prescribing probably won't get you in trouble (but still isn't a great idea). As long as you are not practicing outside the scope of your training and experience, you usually won't be faulted. If you provide negligent care for your family, although in all likelihood they won't sue you, others may report you to your state board of licensure, or an action could be instituted on behalf of a minor. Remember the time-tested adage – *The doctor who treats herself has a fool for a patient.*

Knowledge of Allergies

A no-brainer, but errors continue to occur at alarming rates.

Knowledge of Medications

Do you have a mechanism to ensure that you are aware of all the medications a patient is taking (including nutritional supplements)? A one-page questionnaire that the patient can update at each visit will help make you aware of any changes. This list then behooves you to check for possible interactions.

It is estimated that over 50% of patients take some form of alternative medicine. The PDR publishers offer a volume on dietary supplements. Paperback texts are also available. Many patients are not aware that their "vitamins" are frequently pharmacoactive substances that may well be causing, or at least contributing to, their presenting complaint. Additionally, these chemicals may interact with prescribed medications, and cause untoward outcomes. For example, a _serotonergic syndrome_ can be caused by prescribing an SSRI for a patient you did not know was taking St. John's Wort. If the patient chooses not to reveal such information, this is one matter, but failing to ask is an entirely different one.

Monitoring Medications

Regardless of your specialty, many of the medications you use cause side effects, alter disease processes, and can interact with other medications. You must have some routine for monitoring patients' medications. Again, it is best to brainstorm with your colleagues to find effective solutions. If you have no mechanism in place, you may get a call from the lawyer hired after your patient sustained permanent brain damage from the fall he took (allegedly caused by the orthostatic hypotension that was a prominent side effect of the medication you just prescribed). Your potential liability soars if:

- You didn't warn the patient about this side effect
- You didn't arrange a follow-up appointment
- You didn't take a pre-treatment blood pressure reading

Prescribing For "Ghost" Patients

Anytime you prescribe a medication, you establish a duty to that person. You are clearly safest by never prescribing for "non-patients." If you do, be certain to clearly assess your risks and minimize them. Doctors have lost their medical licenses over "ghost" prescriptions, though this is more likely when controlled substances are involved.

The internet "Viagra®-doc-in-the-box" scenarios are a hot topic. In addition to being liable for negligence (which is difficult to defend if you did not examine the patient – even with the negative cardiac history supplied on the internet questionnaire), you may also be charged with practicing medicine without a license in the state where the patient resides.

Prescribing For Other "Not Really My Patient" Patients

This practice occurs frequently in mental health areas where you have one practitioner providing the therapy, another providing social services, and a physician providing the medication. The duty here is straightforward. You, the physician, have the duty to the patient for the treatment you provide. If a patient commits suicide with the medication you prescribe, your defense of, "but the therapist didn't tell me they were suicidal" will not play well in court. This is why fragmented situations are fraught with risk. Minimizing risk is accomplished with clear communication and documentation. You need to ensure that proper IC is obtained and the patient is educated about his illness and treatment. You need to assess any potential risks and ensure follow-up. Communicate your actions and findings to everyone else involved in the case.

Duties to Third Parties

Ensure you provide a proper warning to patients if you prescribe a medication that may make them drowsy. Your advice should also address not mixing medications with alcohol or other substances (prescription or otherwise). If at all possible, include a family member in the discussion when the patient is elderly or unreliable (though you can't do this against their wishes). In most jurisdictions, you are responsible only for warning a competent person of the potential effects.

Alternative Medicine

Although many practitioners use at least some form of alternative medicine, this is an area of very "thin ice" when doing a risk management inventory. The question you need to ask yourself is as follows: *"If I am sued for allegedly causing an injury from the use of X (an alternative medicine), would the majority of similarly trained, certified, and experienced providers be able to testify that what I did upheld the SOC?"*

If not, be wary – even if you believe what you are doing is innocuous and can "cause no harm." A substance that by itself is not harmful can give rise to a variety of legal claims. For example, remember that any nonconsensual touching constitutes battery (an intentional tort). Again, you should be careful to have written IC for alternative treatments, even if it involves something noninvasive (e.g. accupressure or touch therapy).

The use of herbal medicines and nutritional supplements follows the same logic. If you are practicing family medicine in Germany, where all doctors are trained in alternative and herbal medicines, you will be practicing at the SOC. If you are doing the same thing in Billings, MT, or Augusta, GA, the outcome may be very different.

Check your malpractice insurance policy! In one malpractice case, the physician was sued for negligence after an injury was found to be related to the use of an alternative medicine. His insurance company refused to pay for the damages because the policy had a clause excluding coverage for the use of any drug not approved by the FDA. The doctor argued that the substance used was not a drug. The courts disagreed. The definition of a drug was based on the doctor's intent, rather than on the physical composition of the substance. In another case, a physician's medical license was revoked because he prescribed alternative medicines, even though there was no evidence that an injury was caused by this treatment. The revocation was based on the state statute, in that the doctor "failed to conform to the standards of acceptable and prevailing medical practice." If you do choose to use alternative/complementary medicine, you must ensure that the patient is aware of any available conventional treatment for their condition and that they agree to forgo the conventional treatment.

Technology

The advances made over the past few decades have been tremendous, both in number and scope. As with most advances, problems also arise, necessitating an awareness of the pitfalls. Some examples are:

Telemedicine

Telemedicine is defined as the practice of medicine across distance through the use of telecommunication and interactive video technology. There has been a huge increase in the number of sites using this technology (1,750 in 1993 to 18,766 in 1996). The primary concerns raised about telemedicine are as follows:

1. Who has the duty? There is no simple answer, nor has this been established by case law. Arguments can be made both ways. On one hand, the doctor who provides the care has the duty to the patient. The consulting physician offers advice that the primary doctor can take or leave. On the other hand, if a physician reviews the chart, looks at x-rays, "sees" the patient, provides a consult note, and is paid for this service, many courts would argue that the tele-consultant has indeed established a DPR.

2. What is the SOC? Thus far, there are limited recommendations on standards for physicians to follow in telemedicine cases. The American College of Radiology was the first to establish such standards. Other specialty societies have been strongly encouraged to follow suit.

3. What about licensure? State statutes vary greatly in their wording regarding what constitutes the practice of medicine, and whether they have agreements with other states, or special clauses. Even if a tele-consultant is not found liable for malpractice in a case, he can face both civil and criminal penalties for practicing medicine without a license in many states. Of note, Alabama has one of the most advanced statutes in this regard and offers reciprocity to physicians for the provision of telemedicine services if they are licensed elsewhere.

The licensure issues in telemedicine are similar to those faced by healthplan "advice nurses," toll-free numbers for medical advice, and physician-reviewers for managed care plans.

Electronic Records and Health Information

At the time of writing, federal legislation addressing the many privacy concerns about electronic maintenance and transfer of patient information is pending. States offer quite varied, and in most cases, inadequate protection for the large amount of information now generated and transferred electronically. Some states (ME, MN, WA, CA, MD, RI) have passed, or are considering passing,

comprehensive health information statutes. Some states have strict confidentiality statutes for certain diseases (e.g. HIV, AIDS, mental illnesses).

Legislation will need to balance the legitimate use of the information with the need to protect the confidentiality of those to whom the information pertains.

HIPAA actually required that Congress enact comprehensive legislation to protect electronic health data by August, 1999 (which did not happen). This was extended to February, 2000. There will probably be some legislation passed in 2000 regarding a federal privacy law. The DHHS has recommended that the following five principles be addressed and followed in the body of any law passed:

- Boundaries – disclosure for health purposes only

- Security – health info to be released only with patient's authority to do so (and must be subsequently safe-guarded)

- Consumer control

- Accountability – those who violate the law are subject to criminal punishment and civil recourse (which is the weakest part of current laws)

- Privacy balanced against the priorities of public health

Oops!

What do you do if you've done everything right (or even if you haven't) and something unforeseen happens? There are no simple answers. Frequently, the issue involves an unfavorable or unexpected outcome. A recommended approach (with some caveats) is to empathize with the patient's suffering and express your concern. This is like an apology, but done in a "safer" way. Although the insurance company/risk manager/lawyer, will tell you not to talk with the patient or family when something goes wrong, this may well not be the right advice to take.

"It is not what a lawyer tells me I may do; but what humanity, reason, and justice tell me I ought to do."

Edmund Burke

Most physicians fear that if they tell a patient they're "sorry," it will be an acknowledgement of wrongdoing. While perhaps you shouldn't bare your soul and make profuse apologies, you can, at the very least, acknowledge the patient's suffering.

If the injury is minor, such as an unpleasant side-effect of a medication you prescribed (with adequate IC), you can say something like *"I'm sorry you are so nauseated. We discussed the possibility of this happening but I'm sorry you feel so badly. Let's wait until you feel a little better, and then we'll talk about the other choices we discussed."*

If a more serious, unfavorable outcome occurs, you do not need to go into detail, but you can show the same concern that you would demonstrate if you weren't afraid of being sued. You might say something like *"I understand how badly you feel,"* or *"I wanted to check to see if you needed anything."* If pressed with questions about what happened, tell the person you will get back to her (and do so). You may not avoid a lawsuit, but by showing compassion, you will demonstrate you are not an uncaring monster. Too many physicians have refused to speak with their patients following unfavorable outcomes. In many cases, it is this apparent lack of compassion (or arrogance) that incites the patient to take legal action.

Massachusetts has a fantastic law called the "Admissibility of Benevolent Statements, Writings or Gestures Relating to

Accident Victims." This is better known as the forward-thinking "Apology Statute." This law read, *"Statements, writings, or benevolent gestures expressing sympathy or a general sense of benevolence relating to the pain, suffering or death of a person involved in an accident, and made to such person or to the family of such person, shall be inadmissible as evidence of an admission of liability in a civil action."*

In the above paragraph, an **accident** is defined as "an occurrence resulting in injury or death to one or more persons which is not the result of willful action by a party." **Benevolent gestures** are "actions which convey a sense of compassion or commiseration emanating from humane impulses."

While it is sad to have to legislate compassion for human suffering, this is one of the most eloquent statutes ever passed. It allows physicians to do what comes naturally – provide for the relief of human suffering.

Outside of Massachusetts, while you wait for a similar law to be passed, you must be a bit more circumspect (but no less compassionate).

Caveat
Always look for a way to acknowledge a patient's suffering.

Tools for the High Risk Patient, Family, Situation, and Clinician

The bulk of the following presentation is adapted from the works of Drs. Bursztajn, Gutheil, and Brodsky. An understanding of the types of problems that arise in the relationships between patients/families and their physicians can help avert unfavorable outcomes. In the area of medical negligence, there is no win-win situation once a lawsuit has been filed. In many ways all parties become victims, regardless of the outcome.

The use of the term "high risk" in this section indicates an increased risk of the two "combustibles" – a bad outcome and bad feelings igniting and resulting in malpractice allegations, or other legal action.

First of all, simply having an awareness of a difficult interaction can help you manage the situation in a manner that minimizes your risk. Second, have the names of forensic or consult-liaison psychiatrists handy, either for a formal consult, or to just discuss difficult cases.

The High Risk Patient

There are several different categories of patients where the risk of litigation against medical personnel increases significantly. If there is one characteristic common to difficult patients, it is that they arouse strong feelings (usually dislike) within their caregivers. Once this happens, it is likely that such patients get "tuned out" or unconsciously avoided by the medical staff. Their complaints tend to be minimized, and are not dealt with on an empathic level. Reactions like these from physicians are the very reason that these patients become "high risk."

It is important to identify particular patients (or types of patients) for whom you tend to have negative feelings. This is ultimately more productive than struggling with, denying, or feeling guilty about your negative reactions. Accept them, and use the approach outlined in this chapter.

The Aikido Approach for Difficult Patients

Aikido is a Japanese martial art that teaches its practitioners to use an attacker's energy as the means of neutralization. This approach involves avoiding direct confrontations with angry or difficult people. An Aikido movement typically involves stepping out of the way of an attack, re-directing the energy dissipated by the opponent, and then protecting yourself (and your attacker – this is a gentle martial art). An example of an Aikido-like response is as follows:

Patient: This department provides lousy care! You don't have any decent programs, I rarely see a doctor, and my medication hardly ever gets here on time.

Dr. Aikido: I agree with you – we'd like to see things be a lot different around here. Unfortunately, the cutbacks have affected us as severely as anyone else, and many of the things we used to offer are gone now. There are three doctors away this week, and those remaining are not able to keep the usual pace. The medication has been slow to arrive the last couple of days – I'll look into it for you.

Analysis: It would be easy to respond to the patient's verbal assault with indignation. However, Dr. Aikido knows that the patient, at the very least, is trying to communicate his distress, and that this is valuable information to have. She absorbs the patient's anger by agreeing that the department is not in ideal shape. The staffing situation probably wasn't explained to the patient. Finally, Dr. Aikido acknowledges that the medications haven't been getting out on time, and she'll find out why. At the end of this exchange, the patient knows he's been heard, feels validated for his views, and has that satisfaction that his complaints will be investigated. Take a bow.

The Patient With a History of Litigation

The best predictor of future behavior is, of course, past behavior. If someone has brought a lawsuit against a previous physician, it is much more likely that the person will seek this resolution again if/when things go wrong. Some risk managers recommend you take a "legal history" along with the social history. It may seem awkward to ask "Excuse me Mrs. Plaintiff, have you ever sued a doctor before?" Instead, you can nonchalantly embed questions about legal matters when asking about a list of possible stressors. Knowledge of past litigation shouldn't automatically cause you to practice more defensively. It may perhaps make you a bit less complacent about matters such as complete and accurate documentation, obtaining IC, etc.

The Narcissistic Patient

Narcissistic patients do not typically take responsibility for their imperfections or diseases. If a problem develops, you will be held accountable for the problem. It's important to accept this as a given when dealing with narcissistic patients. Try not to get defensive when they (predictably) question your ability with comments like "Don't you think I should be evaluated by the chairman of the department?" An example of an appropriate response might be "I understand your concerns, Mr. Mirror Mirror on the Wall. The chairman hasn't performed any (name of procedure) in 20 years. She refers all of her special patients to me, but if you'd prefer, we can have someone else review the situation." In doing so, you have recognized the "specialness" (read, entitlement) of the narcissist, and rather than getting into an argument (which you won't win), you have given him the attention and control that he seeks. Remember, arrogance and pomposity stem from an underlying low self-esteem. By understanding that narcissistic behavior is a compensatory mechanism, it is easier to not feel compelled to directly confront it.

The Somatizing or Hypochondriacal Patient

Dr. Murphy will ensure that at some point, one of your patients with chronic back pain will have a dissecting aortic aneurysm; your headache patient will develop a high-grade astrocytoma, and the weak-kneed patient will be diagnosed with ALS. Furthermore, you will miss these diagnoses because you are on autopilot, trying to reassure them that everything is OK. Most physicians learn these lessons the hard way.

Somatically focused patients tend to not bring out the best in their physicians. Nevertheless, they are indeed suffering (usually from low self esteem, multiple resentments, depression, etc.). Somatic symptoms are frequently a defense used to deal with the spectrum of unhappiness in life. Simple reassurance won't work. Instead, treat them like anyone else coming to you for pain control or an obvious disease. Show empathy. Tell them that at this point in time you can't find the cause of their back pain, leg weakness, etc. Make it clear that you understand they are suffering, and that you'll see them in another three months for a checkup. Ask them to keep a diary detailing their symptoms, exacerbating and relieving factors, patterns, etc.

When you see them in three months, be certain to take a look at their carefully kept diaries (it takes little time). In doing so, you are more likely to diagnose a serious illness (when it is present). This also is more of a benefit to patients than simply dismissing their symptoms and ushering them out of the office amid hasty assurances (which are predictably ineffective).

Do not try to provide reassurance by telling a patient that his symptoms are "all in his head." This patient will force you to acknowledge his pain (which subsequently becomes yours), by frequenting the ER, asking for earlier appointments, calling the answering service at all hours, etc. There is a deep-seated fear of abandonment at work in these situations, which can be assuaged with regular, brief appointments.

Caveat

Somatizing patients need to be carefully screened for the presence of depression and substance abuse.

The Noncompliant Patient

You might think that a patient who is a chronic "no-show," or does not comply with your recommendations, is at low risk for litigation. Wrong! Actually, this type of patient may be like the lover who storms out of the relationship, only to become enraged that she didn't have someone running after her. Again, there is usually some primitive pathology at work in the personality realm, coupled with limited insight. This is the very patient who will not show up for her Pap smear, colonoscopy, lab work, etc. The communication that you do receive from her is a subpoena. This is where you need a filing system that will ensure you send reminders to these patients, and if they continue to be noncompliant, discharge such patients from your care. Don't forget to send her a certified letter advising her of the risks she's taking by not attending to her health concerns.

The Doctor, Lawyer, Nurse, or MCO Administrator As Patient

Only Dr. Murphy knows why, but having these people (or their spouses) as patients reinforces the axiom "if something can go wrong, it will go wrong." Furthermore, these patients will be much more likely to know when something actually has gone wrong.

The Patient Who Has Experienced Trauma

As part of a thorough history, it is prudent to ask if the patient suffered from some form of significant past abuse or trauma (childhood sexual abuse, domestic violence, war, etc.). Some people with such histories re-experience current stressors much as they did at the time of the initial trauma. That is, they feel helpless, become enraged, and may unconsciously blame you for both present and past traumas. Again, if you acknowledge their suffering and offer support, you may be able to make a significant difference. Don't overlook the assistance that can be provided by an outside consultant.

The High Risk Family

There are several slightly different species in this taxonomy: families who will project their anger, guilt, prior suffering, resentments, etc. onto you. In each of these situations, the more involved the family is in the treatment process, the less of a problem will result following unfavorable outcomes. Again, don't forget to consider asking for help in these situations (and don't take the criticism personally). A few moments of your time are wisely invested by dealing with the following family situations:

The "Questioning" Parent or Spouse

Beware the parent who second guesses each move you make with his child. In these situations, you need to ensure he understands the reasons behind each of your decisions and gives you proper IC. If there is evidence of discomfort or ambivalence on this parent's part after you have thoroughly explained your findings, consider recommending that a second opinion be obtained before any major decisions are made.

Families of Patients With Somatoform Disorders

The problem in this situation is that the family repeatedly hears the patient say that "the doctor can't find anything wrong with me" or "the doctor doesn't believe me." While the family may well be tired of hearing about the patient's various complaints, if the "big one" actually occurs, they will be the first to point their fingers at the doctor for overlooking an "obvious diagnosis."

The Families of "Difficult" Patients

Many families care for years for someone who is abusive or difficult. This can range from the minor "crotchety" personality to a physically abusive alcoholic spouse. Many of these families have allowed the abuse to continue, and have years of pent up resentment (which will of course be denied if asked about). When something finally happens to dear old dad or dear old mom, the family may react with overwhelming feelings of guilt. These strong emotions can easily be transferred to the attending physician (who may be oblivious to this entire process). Conversely, it is not unheard of that families get angry at physicians for keeping seriously ill family members alive.

Families of Patients With Chronic/Terminal Illnesses

A common variation on the above theme involves a family that is emotionally and economically exhausted when dad finally passes on. It is normal to feel relief in these situations. But like the situation described above, guilt may also arise. Rather than being the helpless target of the projected feelings, the physician can assist the family to discuss and accept grief reactions.

Families That Have Experienced Unexpected Deaths or Unfavorable Outcomes Related to Medical Care

This is a surprisingly frequent situation, in that it is not difficult to be angry at the medical system when someone close to you suffers after being given inadequate treatment. One of the easiest and effective risk management tools you can use is to ask every new patient "Have your prior experiences with healthcare been positive?" Most patients will have something negative to say, and you can respond by saying something like "I'm sorry you experienced that, it must have been difficult for you. Please make sure you ask if you have any questions." In less than a minute you have demonstrated empathy and found out about an aspect of the patient's care that you want to ensure goes smoothly. Many physicians are afraid that asking about unfavorable healthcare experiences can literally open a floodgate. Usually it doesn't. What it does do is demonstrate to the patient that you are willing to listen, and that you value her concerns. These efforts go a long way to establishing a trusting relationship.

High Risk Situations
The ER
The practice setting that has the fewest favorable characteristics is the ER. Patients usually arrive feeling quite ill and may not even be able to communicate. Rarely is the individual's private physician available. Equally rare is the availability of the person's medical record. The ER physician most likely does not know the patient or his family. There is not much that can be done to change the ER situation. Documentation carried with patients (e.g. living wills) is very helpful. If the ER is not too busy, the doctor may get a reasonable chance to speak with the patient and family. The use of ancillary personnel to obtain a thorough history and to provide patient education is a definite plus.

Too Many Cooks
Every time more than one provider is involved in a patient's care, the risk increases for both bad outcomes and bad feelings. The problem usually arises from poor communication between the treating physicians. This can be rectified if one physician (usually the primary care doctor) is recognized as the main contact (sometimes called the "quarterback" of the treating team). With any complicated case, there may be a variety of consultants involved. The designated primary physician must

coordinate all of the information from the different sources, explain conflicting reports (if any), and ensure all the patient's questions are answered satisfactorily.

Lack of Continuity of Care

Another high-risk situation develops when there is no ongoing DPR. Managed care has had the effect of decreasing the time doctors spend with their patients, making it more difficult to establish a therapeutic alliance. If it is not possible to ensure the same physician is seen on each visit, continuity of care can be established by linking patients with nurse educators or case managers.

The High Risk Physician

There are several types of doctors who are at a greater-than-average risk for litigation. The following attitudes and behaviors are particularly discouraged:

The Physician As God

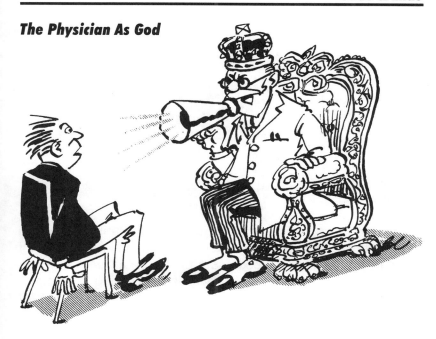

There may be a doctor (or two) who is a tad too arrogant for his own good. This personality type has trouble expressing empathy (and does not understand the need to do so). They tend to intimidate or anger patients, leaving the impression that they really don't care. When there is an unfavorable outcome, there is little hesitation on the patient's part in "getting even" through legal channels. As the old joke goes, "What's the difference between a doctor and God?" God doesn't think he's a doctor – or a lawyer, pilot, surgeon, etc. Unfortunately, narcissism blinds its victims, robbing them of insight into their character pathology. Hopefully those close to such individuals can assist with damage control. Over time, narcissistic doctors can learn from experience, starting with the second lawsuit, or the third. . .

The Physician as Record Keeper

Some doctors are more concerned with what they write in the medical record than what they actually do with patients. As with the narcissistic doctor, the patient is left feeling as if their concerns, needs, and questions are of secondary importance. Some physicians come across this way because they are concerned primarily with avoiding litigation. Others seem to focus on writing in  the record because they are not really comfortable interacting with patients. If you recognize yourself in these descriptions, it is important for your success as a physician to learn to focus on the patient's issues and concerns. Alienating patients is ultimately more detrimental than not having perfect documentation.

The Physician with Guilt

There are some doctors who feel so down on themselves after a situation goes poorly that they beat themselves up trying to understand why things went wrong. They go way beyond the healthy level of "learning from experience," and may go overboard in apologizing to the patient. The patient may actually have been coping well with the outcome – until he sees his doctor so wracked with guilt. This sometimes translates into the following reaction – "Gosh, if my doctor feels so guilty, she must have something to feel guilty about!"

The Defensive Physician

Defensive physicians come across as arrogant in order to defend against their feelings of inadequacy. These physicians also have a difficult time empathizing with patients, and often act in a patronizing manner. An attitude of "How dare you question me?" gets projected, which is not a crowd-pleasing trait.

The Physician Reviewer

Physician reviewers, if they do their jobs well, can balance the needs of the patient with the needs of the organization. Unfortunately, these physicians often get caught in the middle, and may begin to side with the MCO by denying authorization for treatment. More jurisdictions are now holding physician reviewers accountable for their decisions via their state board of licensure, viewing their decisions as no less a practice of medicine than that of the physicians actually treating the patient.

The High Risk Administrator

A good healthcare administrator is a benefit to any organization. A bad one is a huge liability. A competent administrator demonstrates good leadership technique. Through hard work and understanding, they can actually get a "buy-in" from physicians, who will become active participants in the quest to improve quality and consider healthy (and ethical) cost containment measures. The high risk administrator will lead with a dictatorial and threatening style. In no time, the staff start rebelling, and resist many of the

organization's initiatives (especially if they come from Genghis Khan, MHA, MBA). This becomes a very dangerous risk management environment. Any time there is poor morale, risk increases, and everyone suffers.

The High-Risk Physician Executive

This position differs from that of a reviewer, but shares similar pitfalls. This physician is generally the Director of Clinical Services or the Vice-President of Medical Affairs. As such, she is the crucial link between the medical staff and the administration. She can either play a positive and pivotal role in furthering the improvement of quality and involvement of the medical staff, or be a liability.

The clue to which role she will assume is usually evident in the amount of respect this person commanded (as a physician) prior to assuming the executive position. If she possessed leadership skills and was an effective organizer, she can be a crucial link to improving matters. If she achieved success merely through political savvy, and never held the respect of the medical staff, her new position won't change this.

References

Appelbaum PS: **General Guidelines for Psychiatrists who Prescribe Medication for Patients Treated by Non-Medical Therapists**. *Hospital and Community Psychiatry* 42:281-282, 1991

Bursztajn HJ, Brodsky A: **A New Resource for Managing Malpractice Risks in Managed Care**. *Arch Intern Med* 156:2057-2063, 1996

General Laws of Massachusetts, Chapter 233: Section 23D (1986)

Grinfield MJ: **Telemedicine Law Struggles to Keep Up With Technology**. *Psychiatric Times* Aug 1999:20-21

Hilliard J: **Pitfalls of Prescribing Medications**. *The Mental Health Practitioner and the Law*. Harvard University Press, Boston, 1998

Hodge JG, Gostin LO, Jacobson PD: **Legal Issues Concerning Electronic Health Information**.
JAMA 282:1466-1471, 1999

In re Guess, 393 SE2d 833 (NC 1990)

Kaar JF: **Legal Challenges to the Implementation of Telehealth Within the United States and Internationally**.
Legal Medicine 98:32, 1998

Madden J: **What Are The Limits for Drug Company Gifts?**
Am Med News 42:10, 9/6/99

Meza v Southern California Physicians Insurance Exchange.
No CO26203 (Cal Ct APP 3d District, 1997)

Mitka M: **What's In A (Drug) Name? Plenty!**
JAMA 282:1409, 1999

Morreim EH: **Conflicts of Interest: Profits and Problems in Physician Referrals**.
JAMA 262:390-394, 1989

Rodwin MA: **Physicians Conflict of Interest: The Limitations of Disclosure**.
NEJM 321:1405, 1989

Shotwell LF: **Telemedicine and Malpractice: Old Liabilities and New Risks**.
Arent Fox Newsletter Vol 1, www. arentfox.com newsletter, accessed 12/5/99

Studdert DM, Eisenberg DM, Curto DA et al: **Medical Malpractice Implications of Alternative Medicine**.
JAMA 280:1610-1615, 1998

Thomson DF: **Understanding Financial Conflicts of Interest**.
NEJM 329:573-576, 1993

Tran Trong Cuong 18 F.3d at 1135, 1138-1139.

Resources

There are a variety of internet sites that contain very current information on:

- Medical references
- Clinical guidelines
- Risk management tips
- Comparisons of insurance coverage
- State board of licensure for updates
- State statutes on any topic
- Regulatory information

Medical Information

www.pdr.net – in addition to drug information, this site has other resources for physicians, nurses, pharmacists, physician assistants, and consumers

www.igm.nlm.nih.gov – this is direct access for internet Grateful Med (the search engine for thousands of journal articles); it is also accessible through the NIH site

www.nih.gov – provides a wide range of information and provides links to other sites (from bioethics resources to consumer health information); you can connect to both Medline and PubMed for literature searches from this site

www.merck.com – the 17th edition of the Merck Manual (published 4/99) is free for your unlimited online use

www.emedicine.com – an online textbook covering many specialties (only emergency medicine was completed at the time of this writing)

www.ama-assn.org – the official homepage for the American Medical Association offers information for physicians and consumers, as well as a physician locator by name or specialty (even if the physician is not a member of the AMA)

Patient Education

www.drkoop.com – an excellent source for patient information and education on hundreds of topics

Resources

Risk Management

www.jcaho.org – this is the homepage for the Joint Commission for the Accreditation of Healthcare Organizations; it is an excellent site offering many risk management tips (sentinel event alert, how to conduct a root cause analysis) and updated standards

www.ncqa.org – a similar resource offering information to physicians, administrators and consumers on the National Committee for Quality Assurance

www.thedoctors.com – an excellent source for information on medical malpractice insurance (the company is the largest physician-owned insurance company in the country); many good risk management tips can be found here

www.safetycenter.navy.mil – an informative site for those interested in more information on the risk analysis process

Regulatory Information

www.dhhs.gov – provides links to any of the regulatory agencies that oversee medical issues

www.osha.org – provides information on the many safety issues in the workplace

www.usdoj.gov/crt/ada – a good site with more than you could ever want to know about the Americans with Disabilities Act

www.eeoc.gov – the site for the Equal Employment Opportunity Commission; it is easy to navigate with information available on laws for employees and employers

www.nad.org – The National Association of the Deaf; this site offers information for healthcare organizations on translators and appropriate equipment

Legal Information

www.findlaw.com – this site will provide you with many links to legal information (particularly state statutes); you can also get state-specific information by searching for your state bar association

www.mcandl.com – an excellent site offering information on medical malpractice in all 50 states

235

Glossary

These definitions come directly from the author's gray matter and should absolutely not be considered an authoritative source.

Abandonment – the inappropriate unilateral termination with a patient once a duty to that patient has been established; an intentional tort

ADA (Americans with Disabilities Act) – 1990 law with implications for patients, healthcare organizations, and providers

Advance Directives – the legal ability to document what your choices are regarding end of life care that can be used at a time when you may not be competent to make such decisions

Antikickback Laws – several laws which prohibit the payment or receipt of any tangible benefit for the referral of persons to a healthcare facility or the referral to an entity in which the physician or immediate family has an interest

Assault – the threat or fear of unwanted physical contact

Battery – the actual occurrence of unwanted physical contact

Beyond a Reasonable Doubt – proof to a standard of approximately 95% certainty

Boundary Crossing – use of other than strict limits in all nonprofessional relationships with patients; may not (yet) be considered unethical or illegal; frequently leads to boundary violation

Boundary Violation – an unethical and/or illegal personal or business relationship with a patient

Capacity – this is a clinical determination; having the mental ability to make a rational decision (based on understanding and appreciating all relevant information)

Civil Law – has the goal of "to make whole again" (usually by monetary means)

Clear and Convincing Evidence – the need to prove to a jury to a degree of 75-85% certainty; used in some civil disputes where the risks are higher than only financial

Clinical Guidelines – medical recommendations for the evaluation and treatment of specific diseases; if used in an organization, the provider must document reasoning for deviation from established guidelines

Competence – a legal determination; having the capacity to understand and act reasonably

Confidentiality – the clinicians obligation to keep private any information received as part of the doctor-patient relationship

Credentialing – the collection and review of important physician qualifications for practice (including licensure, training, certification, references, etc.)

Criminal Law – has as its goal punishment for offenses committed

Damages, Economic – monetary loss suffered as a result of an injury; may include the following: hospital and doctor bills, lost wages, predicted lost earnings from an injury, etc.

Damages, Non-economic – those non-monetary losses suffered as the result of an alleged injury; includes pain and suffering, loss of consortium, lost quality of life, etc.

Damages, Punitive – monetary fines levied by the court to punish the defendant for their acts/omissions; may be a large sum if a large corporation is the defendant

Defamation – intentional tort of providing/publishing false information that harms another person's reputation, livelihood, relationships, etc.

Defensive Medicine – the use of specific evaluation or treatment measures with the primary goal being the avoidance of litigation (rather than the best interests of the patient)

Deselection – "firing" a physician from a managed care plan

DHHS (Department of Health and Human Services) – a large federal agency responsible for protecting the health of all Americans and providing essential human services; includes the FDA, CDC, IHS, NIH, HCFA

Economic Credentialing – attempts by an organization to apply profiling information on the financial impact a physician has on the organization to the credentialing process; it is always inappropriate

EMTALA (Emergency Medical Treatment and Active Labor Act) – also known as the "anti-dumping law," it requires that anyone who presents to an ER, regardless of their ability to pay, must be medically screened, and then if they have an emergency, treated and stabilized prior to transfer

ERISA (Employee Retirement and Income Security Act) – established to protect employment related retirement benefits

ERISA Preemption – a legal loophole preventing individuals or families from suing a managed care company (recently changing)

Expert Witness – someone with special knowledge of a subject who is called upon to testify; differs from a fact witness (who can state only what they know to be true); expert witnesses can state opinions for the court

FCA (False Claims Act) – law making it illegal to submit any claim to a government agency that may be considered fraudulent

Fiduciary – a position of special trust and confidence, which creates a **professional duty to a patient**

HCFA (Health Care Finance Agency) – agency under DHHS that administers Medicare, Medicaid, and the Child Health Insurance Programs

HEDIS (Health Plan Employer Data and Information Set) Measures – data collected from managed care organizations comparing a variety of preventive and health care indicators used as quality measures

HIPAA (Health Insurance Portability and Accountability Act)

a 1996 law extending insurance coverage and the scope of antifraud statutes

Informed Consent – a legal and ethical requirement to ensure patients fully understand their diagnosis, the risks and benefits of the recommended treatment, the risks and benefits of alternative treatments, and the risks and benefits of receiving no treatment

Intentional Tort – an intentional act that foreseeably will cause damage/harm to another person

JCAHO (Joint Commission for the Accreditation of Healthcare Organizations) – accreditation organization for hospitals, ambulatory care centers, and long-term care facilities

Libel – written defamation

NCQA (National Committee of Quality Assurance) – accreditation organization for managed care organizations

Negligence – covers unintentional torts; to have a case of negligence, all four elements of: duty, dereliction, proximate cause, and injury must be proved

NPDB (National Practitioner Data Bank) – repository of data on all physicians collected since 1990; those registered have had a negligence claim resulting in any monetary payment, received an adverse privileging action, received a negative action from their state board of licensure, or were sanctioned by their professional society

Preponderance of Evidence – a standard of "more likely than not," the requirement to prove to the finder of fact at a level of approximately 51%, this is used in most civil disputes where money is a stake

Privilege – the patient's right to exclude any medical information from being released in a legal setting

Privileging – granting the authority for a physician to practice at a certain facility or with a specified group of patients

Res Ipsa Loquitor – a case of obvious negligence; literally translated this means "let the thing speak for itself"

Respondeat Superior – the master is responsible for the acts of the servants; see also vicarious liability

Risk– the possibility of incurring loss, injury, or damage

Risk Assessment – applying tools to evaluate the risk inherent in specific situations or areas of practice

Risk Management – action taken to minimize risk

Slander – oral defamation

SOC (Standard of Care) – the level of care provided by similarly trained and experienced practitioners under similar circumstances

Standard of Proof – the level of certainty a jury or judge must reach to make a decision in a legal case

Stark Laws – Stark I and II Laws (formally the Ethical Referral of Patients Act); prohibits referrals of patients for medical activities in which the physician has a financial interest

Therapeutic Privilege – an exception to the requirement for informed consent where a physician does not need to disclose all of the information in his possession because it might cause significant physical or mental harm to the patient; used infrequently

Therapeutic Waiver – refers to a patient who waives their right to informed consent stating they do not want to be told about their condition; not recommended

Tort Reform – measures taken at the state and national level to limit the number of lawsuits, inappropriate litigation, and size of awards

Unintentional Tort – an act having an unreasonable risk of causing harm (negligence)

Vicarious Liability – the employer may be legally responsible for the acts of employees

Ten Commandments for Legally Aware Physicians*

I. Thou shalt practice within thy scope of training, experience, and privileging.
II. Thou shalt never place thy needs above thine patient's, and avoideth all personal relationships with those whom you treat.
III. Thou shalt never promiseth a result.
IV. Thou shalt document what thou hast done (concisely, precisely, and legibly).
V. Thou shalt ensureth proper informed consent, and discloseth all treatment options.
VI. Thou shalt maketh every attempt to listen to thine patients and attempt to empathize, even with the unlikable.
VII. Thou shalt ensureth proper professional liability insurance coverage (which includeth administrative actions).
VIII. Thou shalt consult with legal counsel at all times when it is appropriate to do so.
IX. Thou shalt demonstrate humility.
X. Thou shalt knoweth thine state laws and local policies.

This page may be copied and freely circulated

* From the book:
**Medicolegal Issues in Clinical Practice:
A Primer for the Legally Challenged**

by Deborah J. Wear-Finkle MD, MPA
ISBN 1-894328-08-6
Published by Rapid Psychler Press

Index

The Author

Deborah J. Wear-Finkle, MD, MPA is a forensic and aerospace psychiatrist with a consulting practice in Pensacola, FL. She is a Diplomate of the American Board of Psychiatry and Neurology, being Board Certified in General and Forensic Psychiatry. She is fully trained in internal medicine.

Dr. Wear-Finkle is a member of many professional societies, including the American Academy of Psychiatry and the Law, the American College of Healthcare Executives, the American Society of Healthcare Risk Management, and is an associate member of the American Bar Association. She is a faculty member of the Naval Operational Medicine Institute (NOMI), and is responsible for training residents in aerospace medicine and student flight surgeons the scope of aerospace and operational psychiatry. At NOMI, she is the Chair of the Executive Committee of the Medical Staff. She is a Diplomate of the American College of Healthcare Executives, as well as a Certified Legal Consultant. Dr. Wear-Finkle lectures widely on the subject of medicolegal issues.

The Artist

Brian Chapman resides in Oakville, Ontario, Canada. He was born in Sussex, England and moved to Canada in 1957. His first commercial work took place during W.W. II when he traded drawings for cigarettes while serving in the British Navy. Now retired, Brian was formerly a Creative Director at Mediacom. He continues to freelance and is versatile in a wide range of media. He is a master of the caricature, and his talents are constantly in demand. He doesn't smoke anymore.